Using ICT in Primar~   Teaching

Using ICT in
Primary Humanities Teaching

Graham Jarvis

LearningMatters

First published in 2003 by Learning Matters Ltd.

British Library Cataloguing in Publication Data
A CIP record for this book is available from the British Library.

ISBN 1 903300 91 6

Cover design by Topics — The Creative Partnership
Text design by Code 5 Design Associates Ltd
Project management by Deer Park Productions
Typeset by PDQ Typesetting
Printed and bound in Great Britain by Bell & Bain Ltd, Glasgow

Learning Matters Ltd
33 Southernhay East
Exeter EX1 1NX
01392 215560
info@learningmatters.co.uk
www.learningmatters.co.uk

Contents

About this book

This book has been written for primary trainee teachers and Newly Qualified Teachers (NQTs). Subject leaders and Learning Support Assistants (LSAs) may also find it useful. It is for all who want to use Information and Communication Technology (ICT) to enhance the teaching and learning of history, geography, RE and citizenship.

For those of you training as primary teachers, there is a requirement to meet the Standards identified in DfES Circular 02/02, where ICT is identified as both a subject and a support to effective teaching. This book focuses on using ICT effectively in your teaching of the four subjects identified, although it is hoped that its ideas and suggestions can be transferred to teaching in other subjects.

For NQTs your college course and school-based training placements will have had elements which focused on developing your personal ICT skills and capability as well as using ICT in a classroom context. By the end of your course or induction year you will be required to pass the QTS skills test in ICT. The ideas in this book are designed to support and develop your use of ICT during your course and as you move on to a career in teaching.

Subject leaders in one or more of the four subjects can use this book to identify ideas for incorporating ICT into their subject area as well as supporting other colleagues. LSAs who work with teachers in using ICT, or who want to enhance their knowledge and understanding of how ICT can support teaching and learning, will also find the book invaluable.

Content and structure

This book focuses on the use of ICT to support teaching and learning in the humanities. The statutory requirements are found in the National Curriculum for each subject and for ICT. Since a majority of schools now use the QCA schemes of work for their planning, these are used in this book to focus activities for both the subject areas and ICT. However, there is no reason why the activities could not be used in schools that have developed their own medium-term plans.

Chapter 1 sets the scene and identifies the potential for using ICT to support teaching and learning in the humanities. Chapter 2 focuses on geography and uses four units from the QCA scheme of work to identify the potential for using ICT in each. Ways in which teachers could use ICT are described and those tasks where children have 'hands-on' experience are identified. Example lesson plans identify the teaching objectives, activities and learning outcomes and include wider aspects you should consider.

Chapters 3–5 follow a similar pattern for each of the other humanities subjects – history, RE and citizenship. Where applicable, reference is made to research and reasons suggested for using ICT in specific contexts. Web resources are included and suggestions are made for using ICT in a range of contexts with different levels of resourcing. The main focus is on the use of computers, associated software and peripherals, but wider aspects of ICT use are included where appropriate.

Chapter 6 is based upon frequently asked questions about supporting the activities described. Skills that are needed to carry out the activities are identified so the tasks are accessible. Useful websites and other resources are included, relating to each of the subjects and units covered.

Using the book

- Use the subject chapters to support the units you are to teach.
- Select those ICT opportunities that you could use to support your teaching, the children's learning, or both.
- Check what ICT hardware, software and peripherals are available in your school.
- Use and adapt the lesson plans to your own situation.
- Plan and prepare the ICT you will use.

After teaching a lesson, use the following questions to help evaluate your use of ICT and how you might use the book to support you in future lessons.

- Did it help support your teaching?
- Did it support your teaching objectives?
- Which aspects were effective?
- Which aspects would you change in the future?

Background

ICT may have gained a very high priority under the present government but it is certainly not new to schools. The first computers in primary schools were the BBC 'B' computers in the early 1980s. These spawned the Archimedes, which were followed by Acorn RISC PCs. At the same time some schools were also buying Apple computers. During the early to mid 1990s Microsoft and the Windows operating system expanded and the PC platform became the norm rather than the exception, although Acorn and Apple computers can still be found in some schools.

The investment in ICT in the last five years has been vast, with sums totalling in excess of £1.5 billion from the government. There are more computers in primary schools than ever before with latest figures showing that there is one computer to every nine primary children, and 90 per cent of all schools being connected to the Internet.

However, it is not education that has led the way in ICT developments. It is the global expansion of new technologies which has influenced most areas of our lives. Mobile phones and the Internet give us means to communicate quickly and easily with people anywhere in the world. This has led to what has become known as 'e-commerce' where international barriers in trading have been broken down, which in turn has increased the number of private users. Recent estimates suggest the number of Internet users has increased by nearly 80 per cent over the last two years, with half of all users living in North America, 26.1 per cent in Europe and the Asia-Pacific region accounting for 19.9 per cent.

The global expansion of IT and associated technology has led the British government and other educators worldwide to invest heavily in ICT in schools to support teaching and learning, as well as preparing students for work. ICT is now a fact of life in our schools and it is up to all those involved in educating children to decide how best to use it in our teaching and the children's learning. Not surprisingly, the government has also sought to identify 'best practice' in the use of ICT in order to show that it can help in raising standards. The ImpaCT2 report is one such piece of research and is cited in Chapter 1.

This chapter suggests how ICT can:

- make your teaching more effective;
- help children meet your teaching objectives;
- benefit you and the children you teach.

Reference to recent research is included to support you in identifying realistic expectations when using ICT. The chapter identifies ways in which you might need to vary your teaching according to the level of ICT provision in the school where you are placed for school-based training, or where you are employed. A checklist for identifying the ICT resources available is included to aid your planning and delivery.

Why use ICT?

The National Curriculum (DfEE/QCA, 1999) is a statutory requirement and has specific requirements for knowledge, skills and understanding in ICT as well as including ICT opportunities in all curriculum subject teaching. Using ICT to support subject teaching and learning is a requirement in subject teaching at Key Stage 2 but it is left to the teacher to decide when ICT is included at Key Stage 1.

If you are a trainee teacher or newly qualified, you need to meet the Standards identified in *Qualifying to Teach* (DfES, 2002). These require you to show 'sufficient understanding of a range of work in ICT' and that you know 'how to use ICT effectively, both to teach your subject and to support your wider professional role'.

Whether you are a trainee teacher, newly qualified teacher, a subject leader or have a support role in a school you will be expected to look for opportunities to use ICT in subject teaching. You should be able to justify the choices you make and evaluate how the use of ICT has impacted on your teaching and the children's learning. To support your evaluations a pro forma is included later in the chapter. Beyond the statutory requirements you should develop your own skills, knowledge and understanding of how ICT can support you in your school, with your class, and with the resources available.

Personal skills in ICT enable you to access various aspects of the hardware and software available to you. Knowledge and understanding of using the technology in a classroom context gives you the opportunity to transfer your personal skills into your teaching situation. ICT can seem more complex and appear to need more knowledge and understanding than using a big book in literacy, slopes and ramps in science, or cubes in mathematics. Your own confidence and skill level will affect how you perceive ICT before you try to justify and rationalise its use in the classroom.

The level of resources in your school is likely to have a significant impact on whether you choose to use ICT and the ways in which you, or the children, can use it. Whatever your situation you should justify why you believe ICT should, or should not, be used in a particular context with a specific subject. The justification for using any resource is to enhance your teaching and make it more effective. You want your children to learn, and anything that helps that to happen is worth incorporating into your teaching. If you know what the technology can and cannot do then you will be able to select the appropriate applications and tools to support teaching and learning. In this chapter general principles are identified whilst the following chapters will focus on the subject-specific use of ICT.

When asking 'Why use ICT?' to support teaching and learning the principles will be the same as choosing other resources.

- Will it make my teaching more effective?
- Will it help the children learn what I want them to learn?
- What benefits are there in using ICT?

The questions are unlikely to yield 'yes' or 'no' answers because teaching has so many variables. It involves a whole series of complex actions, reactions and interactions between you, the class, individuals and groups. It also involves the physical environment in which you teach, the resources available, the strategies you use and your own teaching style. Whilst recent research identifies positive aspects of using ICT it also reflects the complex nature of teaching and learning and the difficulty in suggesting ICT alone is a deciding factor in enhancing teaching and learning.

In a paper presented to the Scottish Education and Teaching Show (Glasgow, 2001), Peter Rudd of the National Foundation for Educational Research suggested:

> Whilst the ideal would be to establish causal links or positive correlations between ICT inputs and learning outcomes this is difficult, and sometimes impossible, because of the multiplicity of variables impacting on student outcome.

Other research suggests that ICT can be a contributory factor in raising standards when it is supported by 'effective pedagogical approaches and effective teaching strategies' (BECTa, 2001).

The key is to integrate ICT into your classroom practice because it will help the children learn and enhance their knowledge and understanding, and is not just an 'add-on'.

Will ICT help the children achieve the learning objectives?

ICT in itself will not help children learn any more than giving a book to a child will help him or her learn to read, or pushing a child in a swimming pool will teach them to swim. Planning and preparation of lessons are key in identifying what you want the children to learn and how this is to be achieved. During the planning stage you will need to decide if ICT is to be used by you or by the children, or both. If the lesson is to involve children using specific software, accessing the Internet or the use of other ICT tools then you must familiarise yourself with those aspects. You will need to make sure you know the software, have planned the children's route to specific websites, or be familiar with and know how other applications and tools will support the lesson objectives. Primary and other commonly available software have similar functions and tools with which you may already be familiar but some you may have to learn before teaching them to the children. Ensuring the children have the necessary skills to support their learning will avoid annoyance and frustration and make the use of time much more efficient.

There is no magic formula for getting children to learn but with careful planning and preparation, the choice of appropriate resources, effective class organisation and management, knowledge of the children and your skills as a teacher there is emerging evidence that ICT can be effective in enhancing learning.

RESEARCH SUMMARY

ImpaCT2 is an investigation carried out by BECTa for the DfES into the impact of ICT on educational attainment in the UK. In its conclusion it says:

> *There is evidence that, taken as a whole, ICT can exert a positive influence on learning, though the amount may vary from subject to subject as well as between key stages, no doubt reflecting factors such as expertise of teaching staff, problems of accessing the best material for each subject at the required level, and the quality of ICT materials that are available.*

Research carried out at Newcastle University in 1999 in Ways Forward with ICT: Effective Pedagogy using Information and Communications Technology for Literacy and Numeracy in Primary Schools concluded that it is possible for teachers to raise attainment of pupils in their classes when using ICT to support particular objectives. It identified factors that are effective in improving standards of attainment:

- *Clear identification of how ICT will be used to meet specific objectives within subjects of the curriculum to improve pupils' attainment.*
- *Ensuring that pupils have adequate ICT skills to achieve subject specific objectives.*
- *A planned match of pedagogy with the identified purpose of ICT activities and learning outcomes (e.g. by the teacher's use of ICT to demonstrate or model learning rather than pupils' use).*

- *Matching starting points for development for particular teachers in accordance with their preferred teaching styles and approaches.*

Although this research focused on literacy and numeracy, it offers principles that can be applied to the teaching of humanities.

Evaluating your use of ICT

Translating your planning into classroom practice is vital in ensuring the children's learning is focused. The following statements should help you reflect on your planning and lessons taught where ICT has been an integral part. The process should help you to identify 'next step' teaching and have a clearer understanding of the potential of ICT.

The context and planning stage
- The age of the children.
- The subject being taught – what will you use to identify teaching objectives? (QCA scheme of work, National Curriculum, school scheme of work?)
- Previous ICT experience of the children. (QCA scheme of work units, National Curriculum programmes of study for ICT, school scheme of work?)
- Resources available (hardware, software, computer suite, classroom computers, OHPs, data projectors, interactive white-boards).
- Which resources will you use? (Which will best support your teaching objectives and help the children's learning?)
- Will you use ICT to introduce, develop and/or conclude the lesson?
- Are the children to be involved in using the computers?
- How will the children be organised? (Individual, pairs, whole class?)

Reflecting on the lesson
- If you used ICT to introduce, develop and/or conclude the lesson did you believe the use of ICT to be effective? What evidence do you have?
- If the children were involved in using ICT did its use support your teaching objectives in the subject? What evidence do you have?
- Was your organisation of the children successful? What would you change in the future?
- Did the use of ICT have a negative effect on the children's learning? What reasons can you give and what evidence do you have?
- Was the use of ICT a barrier to meeting the subject teaching objectives? (Children did not have the necessary ICT skills, there were problems with the hardware/software, and so on.)

- What have you learned about using ICT in this context? (Your personal skill level needs to be developed, the children need a greater skill level to carry out the tasks set, the use of ICT was enjoyable for you/the children, the use of ICT was motivating for the children.)

What benefits are there for teachers and children?

ICT does not necessarily provide benefits to teachers and children by itself, and the research would seem to support that view. The report, *Primary Schools of the Future-Achieving Today* (BECTa, 2001), suggests some aspects which are likely to increase the benefits from ICT use.

- *Level and type of pupil and teacher ICT training and skills.*
- *Pedagogical awareness among staff.*
- *Staff attitude towards ICT.*
- *The integration into classroom practice and existing teacher interventions.*
- *Pre-use and planning.*
- *School ethos.*
- *Technical support, resource management and infrastructure.*
- *Establishing clear learning and curriculum objectives.*

You are central to children's learning. During the lesson your interaction with the children and the questions you ask are crucial in scaffolding the learning. If you plan lessons with clear objectives where ICT supports those objectives, children are more likely to learn through lessons that are motivating, interesting and enjoyable.

Computers can encourage collaboration and support in the learning process whilst clearly planned tasks can develop independent learning. Finding information and looking for evidence through the use of CD-ROMs and the Internet supports learning whilst meeting differentiated needs. Structured learning activities enable children to focus on particular aspects of the subject whilst the use of open-ended and more challenging tasks enable more able children to extend their learning through a variety of media. Pre-prepared learning routes such as the use of 'web trails' or electronic worksheets can meet different skill levels and variations in the knowledge and understanding of concepts. The outcomes of the children's learning can be presented in a variety of ways through a wide range of ICT resources, which include databases, spreadsheets, word-processing, desktop publishing (DTP) and graphics.

Software programs and websites can be evaluated for the readability of their content, ease of use and intuitiveness. The following site provides guidelines for such evaluations: **www.becta.org.uk/ technology/software/curriculum/evaluation1.html**

Resourcing

The benefits of ICT will arise from a combination of factors but the level and range of resources could have a considerable impact. The number and range of ICT resources in primary schools still varies quite considerably despite heavy government investment. Some schools have set up computer suites with data projectors and interactive whiteboards whilst others have chosen to place a greater emphasis on computers in classrooms or to have laptops. Some schools are still in the decision-making process and will not have reached a high resource level.

Whatever situation pertains to your school it will be the decisions you make about what to use, and how to use it, which will influence the effect on teaching and learning. Access to a laptop, a data projector and an interactive whiteboard will affect the pedagogy and teaching strategies you employ. A computer suite with Internet access and a range of software will enable a range of organisational strategies, whilst limited computer access will mean you need to be more creative in using limited hardware and software with the children.

The following list is included to help you audit the resources available.

Resources audit
A computer, or computers, in the classroom without Internet access
Classroom computer, or computers, networked and connected to the Internet
A computer suite networked and linked to the Internet
A range of software – both 'stand alone' and site licences
Data projector(s)
Interactive whiteboard(s)
Digital camera(s)
Scanners
Use of email
TV, video, DVD and radio resources
Electronic and programmable toys
Video conferencing facilities
Laptops for staff and/or children's use
Printing facilities – colour and/or black and white
Other – a useful section as further hardware and software are purchased

If the school has a computer suite it will almost certainly be timetabled, as may other resources such as digital and video cameras and scanners. Where the computers are linked to the Internet the school will have a policy for its use. Access to a local authority learning network will also affect the policy and protocols for Internet access and use.

You should also identify what other ICT resources the school uses:

- What scheme of work is being used? (QCA/National Curriculum/school?)
- Are there any ICT support materials which children might use to carry out tasks away from the computer? (Books, worksheets?)
- Do the software licences allow for you to take them out of school to review their content?
- Who is the ICT co-ordinator?

The range of ICT applications and tools for teaching and learning in the humanities

Both here and in later chapters I use generic terms for the software applications rather than identify specific programs. (Whilst *PowerPoint* is probably the most well known and used presentation software program, there are primary software suites with similar tools and functions.) Chapter 6 identifies specific software companies and their websites.

Collecting a large amount of data and saving it
During children's work they may collect a number of pieces of information, data or graphics. By learning how to save to an area of the computer, a floppy disc or CD the children can build up a resource which they can access in future lessons. Any information, data or graphics can be edited or discarded as appropriate. Databases can be set up and word-processing, DTP or presentation software used to enable children to communicate what they have learned.

Plotting graphs from spreadsheets
Data collected in numerical form and entered into spreadsheets can be used to generate graphs of different types depending on the data entered. Software that allows children to produce spreadsheets, graphs and text on the same page is both useful and appropriate.

Graphics
Basic drawing programs, clipart on disk and that provided with software applications, pictures from digital cameras, pictures downloaded from the Web and scanned pictures are all ways in which graphics can be used with children. The pictures can be used to enhance work, to find out information, to present secondary resources and be incorporated into their writing. More advanced graphics programs enable children to change and edit their pictures as appropriate. Always remember that whilst ICT can enhance the

look of the work it should not mask the content and what the children are learning.

Presenting text and graphics in a variety of ways

Word-processing, DTP and presentation software enable teachers and children to incorporate both text and pictures. Pictures can enhance the text and text can be used to describe or support the use of the pictures. Pictures can be sized and moved whilst text can be changed through the use of colour, size and different fonts to enhance the impact and be appropriate for the audience. DTP and presentation software can help children to present their work in a variety of ways appropriate to the content and include sound and video clips as children begin to enhance their ICT work with multimedia content.

Using e-mail to communicate over distance quickly

E-mail is probably the most used tool in computing. Being able to communicate over large distances very quickly can be very useful for children. Links to schools or children in other parts of the UK or the world can help children find information to support their work. They can find out about where other children live, the climate, their diet, their beliefs and culture. E-mailing, and getting responses from an 'expert', is a way to add to children's learning.

The use of the Internet

The Internet links millions of networks all over the world with millions of documents accessed through the World Wide Web. Using this resource in schools enables teachers and children to access huge amounts of information to support teaching and learning in these subjects. The *careful* selection of web pages can enable information, pictures, sound and video clips to be viewed and used. When it is appropriate resources can be downloaded into a program and used to support teaching or be incorporated into the children's work.

The BECTa site **www.becta.org.uk/technology/software/ curriculum/evaluation1.html** identifies things you should look for when choosing a website's suitability for the children you teach.

The revision of ideas in word-processing, DTP or presentation software

The use of the cut, copy and paste tools in software applications is very useful when children want to produce first drafts of their work and redraft them or edit them later. ICT enables children to be very creative and, as with many creative activities, there are stages of development. Original ideas may need to be changed or edited. Using ICT can enable each step to be saved. This shows the processes that the child has gone through to reach a finished piece of work. Work in these non-core subjects can lend itself to the development of ideas over time. Different stages can be revisited and refreshed. Ideas can be changed and new ideas proposed.

Presenting work for different audiences

Appropriate software enables you and the children to produce and present work for different audiences. Several software programs enable communication through text, text and graphics, posters, cards, invitations and other formats. Presentation software is based upon a number of slides which you can use to introduce, develop or conclude lessons. Children can present their work to other children, classes or the whole school at assembly time. Children can contribute to the school website as their skills develop.

Encouraging higher-order thinking skills

The use of the Internet and CD-ROMs requires children to analyse, evaluate and interpret the information given. This involves higher-order thinking skills and this needs to be taken into account when setting tasks.

An administration tool

Monitoring, Assessment, Recording, Reporting and Accountability (MARRA) are an integral part of being a teacher. The use of computer software to keep records of the assessments is a very useful tool to monitor children's progress over time and report to parents. Using computers to prepare lesson plans, materials and resources can save time and aid presentation. ICT can be used to record objectives which have been met and to identify progress. The National Curriculum for ICT includes attainment targets. These provide a framework for assessing children's progress in ICT, and apply to the range of tasks and activities suggested in this book.

When deciding what aspect of ICT to use it is worth remembering this statement from the previous National Curriculum for ITT (Circular 4/98): 'Trainees should know when, and when not, to use ICT.' Knowing what tools ICT can offer us makes this decision that much easier.

Conclusion

- ICT is a requirement within subject teaching at Key Stage 2 but at Key Stage 1 teachers should decide how and when to use it.
- ICT skills, knowledge and understanding are a requirement for the award of Qualified Teacher Status.
- ICT can support teaching and learning in the humanities when it is based upon clear teaching objectives.
- Planning and preparation are crucial to making effective use of ICT, as is the role of a knowledgeable teacher.
- The levels of resourcing in the school will affect what you can do and how the children can use ICT.
- It is important to know your skill level as well as that of the children.

Further reading

BECTa (2001) *Primary Schools of the Future – Achieving Today.* Coventry: BECTa.

BECTa (2002) *Connecting schools, Networking People 2002, ICT Practice, Planning and Procurement for the National Grid for Learning.* Coventry: BECTa.

BECTa (2003) *Primary Schools – ICT and Standards: An Analysis of National Data from Ofsted and QCA by BECTa.* Available at **www.becta.org.uk/research**

DfES (2002) *ImpaCT2: The Impact of Information and Communication Technologies on Pupil Learning and Attainment.* London: DfES. Available at **www.becta.org.uk/research/impact2**

DfEE (2000) *National Curriculum Handbook for Key Stages 1 and 2.* London: DfEE.

DfEE (2000) *Information and Communication Technology: Scheme of Work for KS1 and 2.* London: DfEE.

DfES/TTA (2002) *Qualifying to Teach: Professional Standards for Qualified Teacher Status and Requirements for Initial Teacher Training.* London: DfES/TTA.

DfES/TTA (2002) *Handbook to accompany the Professional Standards for Qualified Teacher Status and Requirements for Initial Teacher Training.* London: DfES/TTA.

Moseley, D., Higgins, S. et al. (1999) *Ways Forward with ICT: Effective Pedagogy using Information and Communications Technology for Literacy and Numeracy in Primary Schools.* Newcastle: University of Newcastle.

Useful websites

www.becta.org.uk/research/
BECTa research and other reports.

www.teach-tta.gov.uk
Teacher Training Agency

www.standards.dfes.gov.uk
The Standards Site

www.becta.org.uk/technology/software/curriculum/evaluation1.html
Software and website evaluation from BECTa.

For both key stages the National Curriculum identifies four headings which relate to the knowledge, skills and understanding to be taught:

- geographical enquiry and skills;
- knowledge and understanding of places;
- knowledge and understanding of patterns and processes;
- knowledge and understanding of environmental change and sustainable development.

(The National Curriculum can be accessed at **www.nc.uk.net/Gg-home.htm**)

Good practice in geography is identified as encouraging:

- enquiry-based learning;
- applying new skills in new situations;
- problem solving and creative activities.

The National Curriculum also mentions the contribution that geography, and the other humanities subjects in this book, can make to the 'wider curriculum' and makes specific reference to the use of ICT.

Geography and ICT

The requirement to identify and use ICT only applies at Key Stage 2. At Key Stage 1 teachers are asked to 'use their judgement where it is appropriate to teach the use of ICT'. It is very important that you know what you want to teach and the children to learn in the geography lesson or lessons. It is only when you know these things that the choice and use of ICT is likely to be most effective.

The focus for each lesson or group of lessons is geography and the use of ICT is designed to support the teaching and learning. The word 'support' is important in the context of the ideas and activities in this and the next three chapters. ICT can support the teaching of geography in a range of areas, including:

- enquiry and research-based learning;
- links to local and distant schools;
- access to photographs and maps;
- information relating to culture, diet and food;
- the weather;
- the flora and fauna of different environments;
- cross-curricular links through the history, art and music of places;
- stories of different cultures;
- famous people.

You will need to take into account the children's existing skills, knowledge and understanding in geography and, where you decide to use ICT, the skill level and previous experience of the children.

Three units from the QCA scheme of work cover both Key Stages 1 and 2 and the 'Passport to the world' unit can be taught from Year 1 up to Year 6. Suggested ideas should be transferable to other units and enable ICT to be integrated into your teaching. The four units chosen in this chapter are as follows:

- Where in the world is Barnaby Bear? (Unit 5, Years 1–2)
- A village in India (Unit 10, Year 4)
- The mountain environment (Unit 15, Year 6)
- Passport to the world (Unit 24, Years 1–6).

Unit 5: Where in the world is Barnaby Bear?

Barnaby Bear is a trademark and copyrighted by the Geographical Association. He is used in Unit 5 of the QCA scheme of work for geography to enable children to access the concept of place, their location, maps, physical features, the weather and types of transport. The QCA scheme of work for Barnaby Bear can be found at **www.standards.dfes.gov.uk/schemes/geography/geo5?version=1** Both the Geographical Association and the BBC have sites where you can find out more about Barnaby as well as having shops where you can buy the bear or other supporting resources (see **www.bbc.co.uk/schools/barnabybear/** and **www.barnabybear.co.uk/**).

To use Barnaby Bear you will need to organise children, parents, teachers, learning support assistants or others to agree to take Barnaby when they visit places or go on holiday. The places that Barnaby visits could be in the near locale, a UK town or city, or a holiday in the UK or abroad. The real key is to explain to Barnaby's 'carer' what it is you are trying to teach.

The purpose of this section is to identify the ICT opportunities that are presented by using Barnaby Bear in order to develop children's skills, knowledge and understanding of geography.

The teacher and ICT

Introductions to lessons on Barnaby Bear using projectors and interactive whiteboards will enable you to share the objectives with the whole class and demonstrate what you want the children to do and the skills they will need to use. If at all possible, try to involve the children in using the whiteboard themselves. Pre-prepared information about Barnaby's travels can be shared with the whole class. Pictures of places he has visited (or will visit) or large maps can be shown in this way. As the lesson develops the whiteboard software will allow you, or the children, to add further information or annotate what is already there. This can be saved for future reference or discussion. If the school does not have such resources but you have access to a computer it is still possible to use software to prepare the lesson, print out the slides or pages and then photocopy them onto OHP acetates. Using ICT in this way enables your introductions to have more impact and gives variety to them. Whatever the level of resourcing in your school it is still possible to model effective use of ICT for the children.

ICT opportunities

- Scan photographs of Barnaby Bear taken with an ordinary camera into a computer, or import digital pictures directly into the computer. Immediate access to the pictures enables children to use the images in a variety of ways. Set up a diary of Barnaby's travels in a word-processing or DTP program, or use slides in presentation software such as PowerPoint. Combining text and graphics is an excellent way for you and the children to keep a record of Barnaby's travels.

- Arrange for somebody to take Barnaby away for a weekend, in one of the shorter holidays or even on a school residential visit. Use e-mail to speed up the process of keeping in contact with Barnaby. Regular messages can update the children on Barnaby's travels and digital pictures can be attached to the mail. Daily and weekly bulletins could add to the immediacy of the diary can be kept by the children in school and lead to further enquiry, discussions and comparisons.

  Note: in some schools and local authorities it has been decided that Key Stage 1 children will not have Internet access and in this situation it is unlikely they will have e-mail addresses. E-mails could still be received through your personal account at home or at the school.

- Transfer the photographs, e-mails or other messages to word-processing, DTP or presentation software and use in conjunction with a data projector and an interactive whiteboard. Print out text and pictures and add to a display. This could develop and change as Barnaby travels to different places over a period of time.

- Software that allows children to save words and pictures in a word bank gives support to children carrying out writing tasks. Use word banks as a source to develop the children's geographical vocabulary.

- Set up a document with hyperlinks to predetermined suitable sites to enhance the learning and speed up the process. Ask specific questions and guide the children to information where the answers can be found. If you consider that the information on a particular site is relevant but may be too difficult for the children in your class – then you can (subject to copyright) copy text and pictures into a word-processing or DTP program and edit these to an appropriate level.

  Note: if the children cannot access websites you would have to copy those aspects you want to use.

- Use software to collect data and make graphs to facilitate focused learning. Make a simple database where information is collected about different aspects of Barnaby's travels. Access this at a later date to answer questions or refresh previous learning. There are several primary applications which allow children to produce simple spreadsheets and produce block graphs, line graphs and pie charts at the click of a button. A record of the distances travelled by Barnaby could be collected in this way. Graphs of temperatures in different places could also be used to compare the weather in different countries with that in the UK.

Note: ensure the children are at a level where they can interpret any graphs produced.

- If you do not have easy access to the Internet, use Paint or Draw programs for creative work. Children can design postcards and send them to friends when they go on a visit or on holiday. Use CD-ROMs to help children learn about places, locations, the weather, transport systems and other relevant concepts.

- The Roamer or other programmable toys can be programmed through a simple keypad to move to places laid out on a simple mat in the classroom or the school hall. Using the Roamer affords another opportunity to discuss Barnaby's travels.

Links to the QCA scheme of work for ICT

- Using a word bank (Unit 1B)
- The information around us (Unit 1C)
- Writing stories: communicating information using text (Unit 2A)
- Creating pictures (Unit 2B)
- Finding information (Unit 2C)
- Questions and answers (Unit 2E).

The QCA scheme for ICT does not progress children from one skill to another. A Year 2 unit does not necessarily need the children to have covered the content of a Year 1 unit for them to be able to carry out a task. E-mail is identified as a Year 3 unit but you would need to make a judgement as to the suitability for the children you teach.

A LESSON PLAN: WHERE IN THE WORLD IS BARNABY BEAR?

The suggested lesson plan is included to help identify what elements might be included. It is likely that work involving Barnaby Bear will involve more than one lesson and the format suggested could be adapted to any future lessons. You should remember that the lesson plan illustrated here includes a range of possible options but in your planning it would only be necessary to select some of the ICT opportunities.

You are teaching a Year 2 class and the focus is Unit 5: Where in the world is Barnaby Bear? The aim of your teaching is to develop the children's geographical enquiry skills and their knowledge and understanding of places. Barnaby Bear is to be used as the context for your teaching and you have decided that you will take Barnaby on some travels. You need to identify what activities will meet your teaching objectives and the learning outcomes. The objectives and outcomes are identified for both geography and ICT. The activities link geography and ICT together.

Title
Where in the world is Barnaby Bear?

Year group
Year 2

Key questions or foci
Where has Barnaby been? What is it like?

NC references
- Geographical enquiry and skills: 1a, 1d, 2a, 2c, 2d, 2e
- Knowledge and understanding of places: 3a, 3b, 3d

Geography teaching objectives
- To locate specific places by using maps and secondary sources.
- To compare these places with the local area.
- To develop children's geographical enquiry skills.

ICT teaching objectives
To learn that:

- information comes from a variety of sources and can be presented in a variety of forms;
- that text can be selected from a word bank;
- that control devices such as the floor turtle or roamer follow instructions which contain numerical data.

Learning outcomes – assessment opportunities
The children are able to communicate the places that Barnaby has visited and describe how they are different from/the same as the local area using handwritten text or computer software.

The children are able to use geographical vocabulary in their work through word lists or word banks saved in a word-processing or DTP program.

Geographical language to be consolidated or introduced
Street, town, city, plan, map, distance (near and far)

Resources
For teachers: presentation software, data projector, interactive whiteboard, OHP, digital camera.

For children: photographs, maps showing the school and places Barnaby has visited, Key Stage 1 atlases, access to e-mails, word-processing/DTP software.

Lesson sequence

Introduction
- Use pre-prepared slides in presentation software to show Barnaby on his travels and the places he has been. This will involve using a data projector and a PC, or a laptop. In Year 2 it would be appropriate to include places abroad. If you have a low level of ICT resources, use presentation software to produce a number of slides with Barnaby Bear and the places he has visited. Print these out onto OHP acetates that will take colour. Present the introduction using an OHP.
- Use the slides to ask questions: What is this place like? How is it the same as or different to where you live? Can you describe the similarities and differences? What can you see?
- Link the slides with the e-mails. Read them or ask the children to do so, depending on their reading ability
- Link this to your objective that information comes from a variety of sources and can be presented in a variety of forms.

Activities

- Use word-processing, DTP or presentation software to write about Barnaby's travels.
- Include access to photographs taken on the digital camera. These could be accessed through the word bank facility or saved to a folder for ease of access.
- The word bank you set up prior to the lesson could be used to support their writing.
- Provide specific prompts to enable the children to talk about the similarities and differences compared to their local area.
- Provide a floor map for a group to guide a floor turtle or Roamer to different places visited by Barnaby. Introduce ideas relating to distance, near and far.
- Provide photographs of their locality along with those of Barnaby's travels for comparison and discussion.

Conclusion

- The children who have used the programmable toys can talk about their floor map and whether Barnaby has travelled short or long distances.
- Children who have used word-processing or DTP software can save their work to disk. It can then be shown through the PC or laptop and the data projector (high-resource school).
- The children can talk about their work with children gathered round the computer (not ideal because of the size of the screen).
- Print out the children's work and use it with the whole class to talk about Barnaby's travels linked to the objectives and focus of the lesson.
- Children learn to save so they complete their work in a future lesson, or perhaps when they have more information about the travels of Barnaby Bear.
- Other children could use work that has been printed or saved on the computer in the future. This could be for information or for enjoyment.
- Work can be printed out and can contribute to a class display with focused questions.

Using ICT to contribute to the 'wider curriculum'

The use of ICT in this context can support the promotion and learning of key skills such as communication. Depending on the resources available, children can be encouraged to work collaboratively. Carefully structured learning with a variety of ICT tools to record their work would enable effective and differentiated learning opportunities for all children. Technology can provide the vehicle for children to use geographical language in the correct context. The provision of word banks can mean that children who need support in their writing can access the vocabulary and include it in their writing.

Summary

- Having access to a high level of resourcing can make an impact on the approaches to teaching and learning. A lower level of resourcing can still enable ICT facilities and tools to be used to make an impact and enable you to share the objectives with the children.
- Using this geography unit enables the children's ICT enquiry skills to be developed in a specific context.
- Planning and preparation in the use of ICT is crucial.
- ICT allows for children to learn geographical skills, knowledge and understanding at appropriate levels and allows for differentiation.
- Work produced using ICT can contribute to a display on Barnaby Bear.

Unit 10: A village in India

In this unit the focus is the village of Chembakolli in India although there is the expectation that the learning is broadened to other 'less economically developed countries' and places within those countries.

It is likely that the focus of a village in India will be outside the experience of most, if not all, children you are teaching and the learning will be gained from secondary sources and possibly from children in the school or their parents.

At **www.actionaid.org/schoolsandyouth/chembakolli/ chembakolli.shtml** you can download resources and access video clips but you will need to check you have Adobe Acrobat Reader for some of the resources and Quick Time movie player for the video. Also visit **www.standards.dfes.gov.uk/schemes/geography/ geo10?version=1**. Typing 'Chembakolli' into a search engine can yield a number of sites to support this unit.

The teacher and ICT

The QCA scheme of work identifies what 'children should learn' and these objectives can be used to consider how you will use the ICT resources available. The following major headings are the main foci, with subheadings that you can access at the QCA site:

- How can we find out about Chembakolli?
- Where are Asia, India and Chembakolli?
- What do you think it will be like there?
- What is the landscape like?
- What are the homes of the children like?
- What is the school like?
- What is the main type of work?
- How do people sell and trade goods?
- What are the main similarities and differences between our locality and Chembakolli?

This is a Year 4 unit and you would expect the children to have developed skills, knowledge and understanding in geography and ICT from units taught in previous years. If you want the children to know where Asia, India and Chembakolli are, then high levels of ICT resources can help you to ask focused questions. A large map projected onto a whiteboard can facilitate whole-class teaching, with questions and answers as an introduction. A world map can be used to ask the children to identify the position of both the UK and India. A data projector that has a zoom facility can be used to pick out Chembakolli.

Being able to show video clips helps focus on specific aspects and enables focused questions to be asked. When you want evidence of what the children have learned projected maps, pictures and video clips can be reviewed. The focus for future lessons can be identified and, if the children have access to a computer at home, they can be encouraged to carry out further enquiry and research.

A lower level of resourcing can still enable you to print out maps, focus on small areas and download pictures for use in class discussions, developing questions and for class displays.

ICT opportunities

- The Internet gives you access to sites with materials, resources, text and graphics related to Chembakolli. Use these sites to make a resource bank which you or the children can access and use to support the teaching and learning. Put together a presentation to introduce the lesson or lessons, whilst the children can use pre-prepared resource banks to support their writing.
- Put photographs of the local area alongside photographs downloaded from the Internet or scanned photographs from the Action Aid pack (see web reference above). You could use presentation software to produce slides and project large images. An interactive whiteboard will allow focused discussions and annotations to be made. Alternatively, give the children access to the slides on computers in the classroom, or in the computer suite where they would need to be installed on the school server.
- Use the data projector to show maps of locations on which you want the children to focus. In a school with a lower level of resourcing put the pictures onto OHP slides. Being able to show maps enlarged in this way can be the focus for discussion and relate to questions raised.
- Set up a web trail so that children can access information themselves and be guided to find answers. The web trail is a very useful way to structure the information that you want the children to use. An example web trail is shown on page 26 for the unit. A mountain environment.
- Encourage the children to show what they have learned by using word-processing, DTP or presentation software to respond to focused questions such as those taken from the QCA scheme of work. Alternatively, devise your own questions.
- Use software that allows children to draw maps, plans of the area and routes of how to get there. Add supporting text. This combination is an effective form of communication and the children's work can be assessed against the learning outcomes.
- Software that allows picture and word banks to be set up gives support to the work. Ask the children to select appropriate pictures to support their writing and use the word bank to select words that they might find difficult. They might produce a travel guide for the area when they have learned about its various aspects. Other forms of writing could be developed from looking at Chembakolli.

Links to the QCA scheme of work for ICT

You could expect the following areas to have been taught or be part of your Year 4 planning and would support the ICT opportunities identified.

- Using a word bank (Unit 1B)
- The information around us (Unit 1C)

- Writing stories: communicating information using text (Unit 2A)
- Creating pictures (Unit 2B)
- Finding information (Unit 2C)
- Combining text and graphics (Unit 3A)
- E-mail (Unit 3E)
- Writing for different audiences (Unit 4A)

Always check the children have the skills to carry out the tasks you have prepared for them.

A LESSON PLAN: A VILLAGE IN INDIA

You are teaching a Year 4 class and the focus is Unit 10: A village in India. The aim is to build on the geographical enquiry and skills taught in previous units and expand the children's knowledge and understanding of places.

Title
A village in India

Year group
Year 4

Key questions or foci
Where is Chembakolli? What is it like? How are Chembakolli and its people the same as/different from my town and the people who live there? How can we find out?

NC references
Geographical enquiry and skills: 1a, 1c, 1e, 2a, 2c, 2d, 2e
Knowledge and understanding of places: 3a, 3b, 3c, 3d, 3f, 3g

Geography teaching objectives
- To know where Chembakolli is in relation to their home.
- To know the main features of the village and about the people who live there.
- To identify the similarities and differences between Chembakolli and other places.

ICT teaching objectives
- To find out information from the Internet.
- To write for different audiences using specific software programs.
- To use resource banks with words, graphics and hyperlinks to access information and support their writing.

Learning outcomes – assessment opportunities
- Children can use a software program to write about Chembakolli: where it is, what it is like, about the people who live there. Ask them to compare it with their local area and other places.
- Children show they can access information through the Internet and through pre-prepared resource banks and carry out specific enquiries.

Geographical language to be consolidated or introduced
India, Himalayas, Hindi, monsoon, mountain

Resources
For teachers: laptop/PC, interactive whiteboard, data projector, presentation software, digital camera, OHP facilities.
For children: maps, books, atlases, photographs, Indian food, Indian costume, Internet access, DTP software, computer suite (or access to one or two PCs, which may or may not be linked to the Internet).

Lesson sequence

Introduction

Use a data projector and whiteboard so that your introductory input is to the whole class. Large graphics and text can involve the children and lead to a question and answer session.

- What is Chembakolli like?
- What do you notice about the homes in the village?
- What do the people wear?
- Can you tell anything about the weather in Chembakolli?
- How is it similar to/different from where you live?

Alternatively, prepare slides in presentation software and put them onto OHP acetates to help with the impact. Once again, you have control of the learning environment. Put materials onto the server for access in a computer suite or the classroom.

Activities

- Give the children a web trail or ask them to use search engines to find out answers and information relating to Chembakolli.
  - What is Chembakolli like?
  - How similar/different is Chembakolli to their own city/town/village?
  - What jobs do people do in the village?
  - Can you describe the landscape?
- The children could use software to record their answers and write in detail about Chembakolli.
- The children could use word banks to access saved words and pictures to support their writing.
- The school could set up a link with another school in India or another country where the children can exchange e-mails and find out about life in another country.
- The children could use Paint or Draw software to create their own pictures based upon what they have found out.
- The children could use software to present their work to others in the class, or in other classes, or to the whole school in an assembly.

Conclusion

Work on a unit such as this will not be concluded in one lesson so the plenary can be seen as a conclusion to one lesson and a 'jumping-off point' for the next. ICT can be very helpful in this respect.

- Save the children's work to disk, CD or to the hard drive ready for the next lesson.
- Completed, or part-completed work, can form the basis for a discussion on what children have found out. Project and share the children's work with the whole class. (Sharing work on a computer screen would be difficult with 30 children.)
- Print out particular aspects of children's work – their text, graphics or both – and add to a focused display. A colour printer is essential if the benefits of children's work in ICT involve graphics or coloured fonts.
- Children can generate questions which could be the focus for a future lesson or lessons.

Using ICT to contribute to the 'wider curriculum'

In this context ICT enables children to access information about children, homes, schools and other aspects of life in what for most children will be a 'far away country'. Pictures and video clips can help the children get a real sense of life in Chembakolli. This helps support their knowledge and understanding of different cultures and has links into RE and citizenship. Key skills can be developed through the use of ICT and inclusion, and differentiation is supported by the careful selection of appropriate resources.

Summary

- The use of ICT enables children to access information and pictures as a secondary source.

- ICT can enable the lesson objectives to be shared with the whole class.
- Using high -level resources enables pictures, maps and video clips to be shown as a focus for questions and learning.
- The use of ICT can enhance the contribution of geography to the 'wider curriculum'.
- ICT can support the assessment opportunities arising from the children's work.
- High-level ICT resources can help to enhance the impact when introducing a lesson, or to focus on specific aspects.
- Where the level of ICT resources is not so advanced there is still the potential to support teaching and learning through the use of OHTs and other audio-visual resources.

Unit 15: The mountain environment

The mountain environment is unlikely to be an everyday experience for the children unless you are teaching in Scotland, parts of Wales or the Lake District. You may have some children who have visited these regions of the UK or have been to mountainous regions for holidays or to ski. Children who can bring these experiences to the classroom can be a useful resource.

This unit is designed to deepen the children's understanding of this particular environment and will have to be accessed mostly through secondary sources. ICT can be extremely helpful in accessing information, pictures and other resources related to the mountain environment. The QCA unit can be found at:

www.standards.dfes.gov.uk/schemes/geography/ geo15?version=1 Other sites that support this unit are:

www.4learning.co.uk/essentials/geography/units/ mount_bi.shtml (a range of information and graphics as well as links to worksheets, an image bank, a search facility for relevant sites and some interactive parts including a quiz)

www.educate.org.uk/teacher_zone/classroom/geography/ unit15.htm (a large resource to support teaching this unit with lesson plans, a teacher factfile, worksheets and links to other relevant sites).

The teacher and ICT

The mountain environment is described as a long unit in which children are encouraged to learn through 'research' from textbooks and pictures as well as CD-ROMs and the Internet. The unit offers opportunities for the children to follow up research and enquiry in their own time. ICT is specifically identified as being useful in this context. The areas that children should learn are as follows.

- What is a mountain environment?
- Where are mountains found?
- What are these places like?
- How does the weather compare in each of these places?
- What effect does the weather have on tourism?
- What effect would tourism have on the chosen area?
- What would I need to do to plan a camping holiday in this area?

A useful starting point would be based on what the children already know. For example, do children think about a mountain environment as:

- snow-covered all the year round, as on the top of Mount Everest?
- a place to ski?
- a barren place?

Have the children considered what it might be like to live there or what jobs people might do? Other ideas may develop through personal experience, television programmes or Internet sites.

The following suggestions focus on the content of the unit and could be used to introduce it.

- Pictures of hills and mountains for the children to discuss and compare.
- Pictures of different mountains and at different times of the year.
- Questions relating to mountain areas, leading to discussion.
- Pictures and perhaps video clips on mountain weather.
- Using online holiday brochures to help the children consider issues relating to tourism.
- Projecting large maps to identify mountains of the world.

ICT opportunities

- Learning that entails the use of secondary sources to meet the objectives for geography needs both careful planning and a structured approach. A structured approach means that the children are guided and supported through predetermined and pre-planned routes. The following example enables children to find information, answer questions, and communicate their learning. From an organisational point of view it would be sensible to allocate each pair or group of three working on the mountain trail to a specific area. Group findings can be fed back to the whole class and comparisons made between different locations and conclusions drawn. Where the children are asked to CLICK HERE a hyperlink to a suitable site would be included.

A mountain trail

Look at the following pictures. Write what the differences are in the box below.

CLICK HERE for some information on hills and mountains.

Can you name some of the main mountain ranges in the world?

CLICK HERE to find out about mountains throughout the world and then answer the following questions:

Which mountain ranges did you look at?

1.

2.

3.

Put a mark on the world map where these mountains are located:

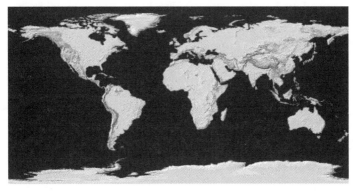

You are now going to find out about one particular mountain range. Use the links below to gather information so you can answer some questions:

The Andes

The Himalayas

Mont Blanc

United Kingdom

The Austrian Alps

From your choice, answer the following questions:

Describe what the mountains are like in our own words.

Why do people visit these mountains?

What is the weather like in this mountain environment?

What work do people do in this area?

Write here anything else you found out.

- A poster is a good way to combine children's ability to present their knowledge and understanding in a way which makes them think about what it is they are trying to communicate and how best they can make an impact. A mountain environment might give rise to posters on:
  – dangerous aspects of which visitors or tourists should be aware;
  – signs to indicate things to look out for;
  – places where visitors or tourists should not go.
  Using Draw or Paint programs the children can draw their own images, include text and graphics and move each or all of them to make the most effective design.
- A database is an excellent way for children to build up records about places. A record of particular mountains or mountain ranges could be set up with a variety of fields in each.
  – The name of the mountain or mountain range.
  – The height of the mountains.
  – The names of people who live in specific ranges and environments.
  – The type of climate.
  – The animals living in a particular mountain environment.
  – The type of tourism that is attracted to a particular area.
  Once the database has been set up it can be used by other children to find out information by asking questions. This 'interrogation' helps the children think carefully about what it is they want to know and can lead to comparisons being made between different mountain ranges. Sharing information and the use of a database enables the children to widen their learning.

- Spreadsheets are useful in collecting information about the heights of mountains, data on the weather or other relevant data. A block graph of mountain heights could compare different mountains in different environments. Data about temperature, rainfall or sunshine hours could be collected in a spreadsheet and a block graph or line graph generated. This could lead to discussions about the most appropriate way to display the information. Graphs projected onto whiteboards, a plain wall or printed out for display could form the basis for further questions and discussions. As children develop their ICT skills the opportunities for integrating ICT into their learning begin to open out and a variety of ways to present their work become available to them. Presentation, word-processing, DTP and whiteboard software can all be used by the children to show what they have learned. If the resources are available, and the skills are developed sufficiently, children can produce trails of their own, which integrate sounds, music and animation. This work can be shared with the class or others in the school and can show geographical knowledge and understanding through creative use of ICT.

Links to the QCA scheme of work for ICT

The mountain environment unit is taught in Year 6 and so you would expect the children to have reasonably advanced computer skills that have been developed during their primary schooling.

- Using a word bank (Unit 1B)
- The information around us (Unit 1C)
- Writing stories: communicating information using text (Unit 2A)
- Finding information (Unit 2C)
- Questions and answers (Unit 2E)
- Combining text and graphics (Unit 3A)
- Introduction to databases (Unit 3C)
- Writing for different audiences (Unit 4A)
- Analysing data and asking questions: using complex searches (Unit 5B)
- Evaluating information, checking accuracy and questioning plausibility (Unit 5C)
- Introduction to spreadsheets (Unit 5D)
- Multimedia presentation (Unit 6A)
- Using the Internet to search large databases and interpret information (Unit 6D).

A LESSON PLAN: A MOUNTAIN ENVIRONMENT

You are teaching a Year 6 class and the focus is Unit 15 from the QCA scheme of work. This example lesson could be used at the beginning of the unit and other lessons developed from it. The National Curriculum references that are given are wide-ranging so it would not be expected that all of these are the foci for one lesson.

Title
The mountain environment

Year group
Year 6

Key questions or foci
What is a mountain environment and where are they found? What is a mountain environment like?

NC references
Geographical enquiry and skills: 1a, 1c, 1d, 1e, 2a, 2c, 2d, 2f
Knowledge and understanding of places: 3a, 3b, 3c, 3d, 3e, 3f, 3g
Knowledge and understanding of patterns and processes: 4a, 4b
Knowledge and understanding of environmental change and sustainable development: 5a, 5b.

Geography learning objectives
- To learn about mountain environments through secondary sources.
- To learn where mountain environments are in the world.
- To learn how different mountain ranges in different places may differ.

ICT teaching objectives
For the children to learn how:

- to research information on the Internet;
- to present their work in different ways depending on the ICT tools and resources available (e.g. word-processing/DTP, databases, spreadsheets, presentation software).

Learning outcomes – assessment opportunities
- The children are able to communicate their understanding of a mountain environment in a variety of ways.
- The children can describe how one mountain environment may differ from another and suggest reasons for these differences.

Geographical language to be consolidated or introduced
Mountain, hill, environment, blizzard, avalanche, crag, peak

Resources
For teachers: data projector, interactive whiteboard, presentation software, OHP.
For children: photographs, maps, globes, books, pictures downloaded from the Internet, word-processing/DTP presentation software, spreadsheets and databases.

Lesson sequence

Introduction
Project a variety of pictures showing various mountain ranges, maps and environments. Use these as a starting point to focus on what the children need to do. Show the mountain trail and how the children can use the Internet to find out information. Ask specific questions as a lead into the children's activities. A video would also enhance the teaching.

Activities
- Use the 'Mountain trail' to access pictures and information from the Internet.
- Use the information to answer questions on the 'mountain trail'.
- Use databases or spreadsheets to record data in order to produce graphs, or to interrogate the database.
- Use appropriate software to present their work.

Conclusion
- Project the children's work onto a whiteboard so their ideas and work are shared.

- Talk about what the children have found out and show 'print-outs' of their work.
- Draw conclusions about the mountain environment based upon the lesson objectives.

Using ICT to contribute to the 'wider curriculum'
- The promotion of key skills using ICT.
- Their learning has been enhanced by using ICT for collecting data and information independently or in groups.
- The use of ICT facilitates learning and recording opportunities at differentiated levels.

Summary
In this context ICT can:

- support the learning of geographical skills, knowledge and understanding related to a mountain environment;
- provide a structured learning path through links to relevant, appropriate and useful sites;
- be used to focus on the objectives for the lesson or a series of lessons;
- facilitate the recording of data and information through the use of spreadsheets and databases;
- facilitate children's ability to record and present their work in a variety of forms.

Unit 24: Passport to the world

As this unit allows opportunities for geography teaching across both key stages, the structure of this section is different from the previous sections. There are no suggested lesson plans but the headings from previous examples could be used. This section looks at the geographical objectives for Key Stages 1 and 2 as identified in the QCA scheme and then identifies the potential for using ICT to support those objectives.

The link for the QCA scheme of work for this unit is at **www.standards.dfes.gov.uk/schemes/geography/geo24?version=1** The QCA scheme identifies questions related to each key stage with subheadings for each. These can be found at the QCA site or in the QCA document. Other useful sites are:

www.4learning.co.uk/essentials/geography/units/passworld_bi.shtml (gives ideas, links to related sites, worksheets and other aspects to support the teaching of this unit)

www.educate.org.uk/teacher_zone/classroom/geography/unit24.htm (provides worksheets, resources and supporting materials).

Geography objectives identified in the QCA scheme of work
Where can I go from my home? *(Key Stage 1)*

What links do I have with other places in the world? *(Key Stage 1)*

How are places similar to, and different from, other places? *(Key Stage 1)*

What can we find out about places from different media? *(Key Stage 1)*

How can we find out where places are? *(Key Stage 2)*

How do we find out about places? *(Key Stage 2)*

What are the reasons for places being mentioned in the news? *(Key Stage 2)*

How are places described in stories? *(Key Stage 2)*

The use of these headings could be helpful to you in identifying ICT opportunities.

ICT opportunities

This unit presents an opportunity for ICT skills to be taught, used and progressed throughout the primary school whilst supporting the geographical aspects of the work. The work could start in Key Stage 1 by discussing the following with the children.

- What is a passport?
- What does a passport have in it?
- What information does it contain?

These questions can lead into children designing their own passport. The idea of the passport could be supported by the use of ICT and the work printed out as a 'hard copy' and made into a book, or it could be made and stored electronically on a computer. Whichever format you decide upon the process will be the same. The aim is not to produce a copy of a normal passport but to create something that is personal and includes information about the child. The children can design a front cover using original work done with a Paint or Draw program or they could import a picture of themselves.

Inside a series of writing frames could be used to help the children write about themselves:

- About me.
- Where I live.
- What I like.
- My family.

Other headings could be added after discussion with the children. A page could also be set up headed 'Places I have visited'. This could include places they have visited most recently and include short descriptions of the place, who they went with, where they stayed, as well as pictures they have from these visits. If a scanner is available, the pictures could be scanned into the electronic version.

As the child progresses through school and moves towards the top of Key Stage 2, more and more pages can be added as they visit more and more places. You could print all or part of the child's passport or save to the computer. Children can use the stored information to think about a range of places, compare them with their home environment, develop an understanding of how they can use maps and the location of the places visited, and think about other aspects which you want them to focus upon. Building up this resource enables you to use the children's own experiences that have happened over time.

As the children's ICT skills develop it will be possible for you to teach the children to use more advanced tools within specific software.

- Using links from one page to another could make electronic books.
- Presentation software is an ideal vehicle for enhancing children's work.
  - Slides can have animation added.
  - Narration can be recorded to accompany the slides.
  - Graphics, pictures and clipart can be added to enhance the work.
  - Short movie clips can be added from digital or video cameras.

The contribution to the wider curriculum is supported by ICT through the teaching and use of key skills and the way ICT can enable all children to access the curriculum and produce work at a level appropriate to their knowledge and understanding. At different ages the children's geographical language can be developed and ICT can be the vehicle for a structured approach to learning whilst at the same time enabling children to be creative and imaginative with the tools available.

Conclusion

This chapter has suggested how ICT can support geographical skills, knowledge and understanding. Ways in which ICT can be used with different level of resources have been identified, as have the possibilities that ICT can offer in supporting teaching and learning geography. Example lesson plans have been given as introductions to QCA units and ideas for you or the children to use ICT.

3 Using ICT to support teaching and learning in primary history

The National Curriculum identifies the knowledge, skills and understanding of history to be taught at Key Stages 1 and 2 under the following headings:

- chronological understanding;
- knowledge and understanding of events, people and changes in the past;
- historical interpretation;
- historical enquiry;
- organisation and communication.

It also identifies the contribution that history can make to the wider curriculum and gives specific emphasis to ICT. You can access the National Curriculum online at **www.nc.uk.net**. Attainment targets identify the levels for ICT against which children's progress can be assessed and can be found at **www.nc.uk.net/nc/contents/ICT- -
-/ATT. html**

History and ICT

History is a subject that is based upon evidence. The main principles of good practice in history are to enable children to look for and question evidence and reach objective conclusions based upon their enquiry and research. ICT is an excellent resource to enable these aims and objectives to be met.

It is possible to identify three strands where ICT can support teaching and learning in history.

1. As a vehicle to help and support the communication of ideas.
2. To help children gain knowledge through enquiry and research.
3. As a support to learning through simulations and role-play.

A range of software is available for teachers and children to record and communicate their ideas based upon evidence, including the use of e-mail. Using ICT as a tool for communication can enable structured learning, support activities and learning away from the computer. Worksheets can be produced where they are part of good practice in history.

History has a knowledge base which children need to be able to access and learn. ICT has a number of tools which can be sources for the extraction of information. CD-ROMs and the Internet are probably the most obvious sources but video, DVD and audio texts provide opportunities to use a wide and varied range of secondary sources. By preparing the materials carefully in advance, focused questions can be identified. The children can make predictions and then use the source, or sources, or information to check whether their ideas could be verified through the evidence. The inclusion of prediction means it is history rather than a comprehension exercise. ICT can also provide a resource bank to enhance your own knowledge and understanding of the subject. School websites are another area where you can find how others have approached this unit.

The third aspect of history teaching and learning where ICT can play a part is that of simulations and role-play. Both of these aspects encourage children to problem-solve and ask 'what will happen if?' questions. Simulation software and programs that involve children in role-play are limited but *Kar2ouche* is one such example. The use of databases and spreadsheets can be used to identify trends and patterns in historical data and to draw conclusions.

The four units from the QCA scheme of work chosen in this chapter are as follows.

- What were homes like a long time ago? (Unit 2, Year 1)
- How do we know about the Great Fire of London? (Unit 5, Year 2)
- What was it like for children in the Second World War? (Unit 9, Years 3/4)
- How has life changed in Britain since 1948? (Unit 13, Years 5/6).

Unit 2: What were homes like a long time ago?

The QCA scheme for this unit can be found at **www.standards.dfes.gov.uk/schemes/history/his2?version=1**

Other sites that support this unit can be found at:

www.educate.org.uk/teacher_zone/classroom/history/ unit2.htm

www.thelighthouseforeducation.co.uk/clicker/flashhistoryks1/ homes.swf

www.qca.org.uk/ca/subjects/english/y1t1_hi_u2.asp

The use of a search engine will also reveal other sites to support you or the children.

The aim of this unit is to help children identify differences between homes today and in the past by looking at their features and their contents, and learning how life in a past time was different from today.

The teacher and ICT

You could arrange a visit to houses near to the school, but you may need to use museums, artefacts and elderly relatives to provide primary sources as well. ICT can provide access to information and pictures whilst the Internet may be used to access 'virtual museums' to provide further information. A data projector for displaying pictures onto a whiteboard or screen can be very effective when looking at all aspects of houses today and through history. The interactive whiteboard allows you to annotate and focus on particular aspects whilst the children can also be engaged in the process. If your school has low-level resource provision you can still copy and project pictures with an OHP as part of any lesson.

ICT opportunities

- Use presentation software to show pictures of 'homes a long time ago'. Their projection can make an immediate impact and provide a focus for a lesson or series of lessons. Large projected images allow children to identify aspects of the houses being displayed. As the unit is for Year 1 it is unlikely, but not impossible, that the children's ICT skills will be developed sufficiently for them to produce something in presentation software.

- Pictures taken of houses in the locality, parts of houses and perhaps artefacts are very useful in bringing the unit 'alive' and help children to have an instant resource in the classroom to which they can refer at the appropriate time. If you do not have these resources, use photographs to add to a display, or an OHP to project images. Video can also be used.

- Use Paint or Draw programs to enable the children to create their own images of houses they have seen during 'fieldwork' or those prepared by you as part of the teaching. The pictures can be changed and edited as the children wish. Text can be added to support your assessment and for 'next step teaching'.

- If first-hand sources are not available, you will need to rely on secondary sources. Books are one source of information but pictures from CD-ROMs and the Internet can provide a rich resource. However, the richness of the resources can be overpowering for children and, where this is the case, selecting specific information and pictures to copy and paste into software enables you to focus the teaching.

- Use software applications to prepare questions for the children. This may be done as a whole-class activity or be used as a support activity after the children have used other sources.

- In the QCA scheme for the unit it is suggested that you read a story set in a Victorian or Edwardian home with pictures of different rooms. Although it can be time-consuming, you can use software to copy a story or write a story of your own. The story can then be enhanced by the use of pictures that you have scanned, copied and pasted, or downloaded (always remember to check copyright issues). Choose the story to meet your objectives, ensuring that the text level and pictures are appropriate to the children you are teaching. The story can be saved and used in the future or edited so that it is at the appropriate level. Software with 'speech options' enables children to listen to the story as they follow it on screen.

- Using a structured learning environment where children can link to pictures, files, documents or websites can ensure the learning time is used efficiently.
- Set up word or picture banks of associated vocabulary or pictures to support children's writing. These could be used by children in word-processing or DTP programs, or might be printed out for children to support their writing away from the computer.
- Although the QCA scheme for ICT does not identify the use of databases until the beginning of Key Stage 2, there is a range of software that enables you or the children to set up simple branching databases. Using a branching database can make the children think carefully about similarities and differences.

A branching database related to the unit: what were houses like a long time ago?

Examples of questions that can be used in a branching database to help children differentiate between different types of houses follow. You will need to consider teaching the skills involved before getting the children to carry out the activity. Getting the children to work away from the computer helps them understand the need for questions that generate yes/no answers.

- Is the house joined on one side? (To separate semi-detached houses from others.)
- Is the house joined on both sides? (To separate terraced houses from others.)
- Is the house not joined at all? (To separate detached houses from others.)
- Does the house have one storey? (To separate bungalows from others – remember they could be detached or semi-detached.)
- Does the house have two storeys? (To separate houses from bungalows.)

As the unit progresses you could devise questions with the children that separate Victorian houses from Edwardian houses, or modern houses, or houses bought at different times (e.g. the 1950s or 1960s) by using carefully selected criteria.

You may decide to use pictures to aid differentiation.

Links to the QCA scheme of work for ICT
- Using a word bank (Unit 1B)
- The information around us (Unit 1C)
- Labelling and classifying (Unit 1D)

- Representing information graphically: pictograms (Unit 1E).

The areas identified above are specifically ones that the QCA scheme identifies as Year 1 units. However, you may decide that the following units could be used as part of your teaching:

- Writing stories: communicating information using text (Unit 2A)
- Creating pictures (Unit 2B)
- Finding information (Unit 2C)
- Questions and answers (Unit 2E)
- Combining text and graphics (Unit 3A)
- Branching databases (Unit 4C).

A LESSON PLAN: WHAT WERE HOMES LIKE A LONG TIME AGO?

The lesson plan is to support the first lesson of the unit and helps identify where you, or the children, can use ICT to support both teaching and learning. Adapt it to meet your specific needs.

Title
What were homes like a long time ago?

Year group
Year 1

Children's previous experience
- Know about history from a previous unit on 'Toys'.
- Be familiar with the computer and able to use the keyboard to type in text.

Key questions or foci
- What sort of homes do people live in today? How can we find out?

History teaching objective
- To talk about/describe different sorts of homes and say/write how they are the same/different.

ICT teaching objectives
- To use software programs to communicate what they have learned about different houses.
- To use software tools to support their writing.

Learning outcomes – assessment opportunities
- Children describe through speech or writing the different types of homes they have found out about. They should describe how the homes are similar and how they are different.

Resources
For teachers: data projector, interactive whiteboard, digital camera, presentation software.
For children: word-processing or DTP software with word bank and picture bank facility.

Lesson sequence

Introduction
Lead a whole-class introduction to set up the unit and subsequent lessons using presentation software, data projector or interactive whiteboard, OHP or display, to show different houses. Ask: what sorts of homes do the children live in? Can you describe them? Look at the pictures — what do you notice? How are they different/similar?

Activities
Children use the word-processing or DTP software to write about different types of homes they have

learned about, using the word and picture banks set up for them to connect specific vocabulary with types of houses. Save the work to the children's folder or floppy disk or print it out. Support the children's use of the word and picture banks to access vocabulary and graphics to be used in their writing.

Conclusion

Use the presentation, OHTs or display from the introduction to involve the children in talking about what they have learned about different types of houses. Ask: what have we learned about different types of homes? How are they different/similar? What parts of the houses make them different/similar? Can you name these different homes? Use children's work, saved to disk, to project onto the whiteboard or a wall so the evidence of learning can be illustrated.

Extension activities

Use pre-prepared questions to extend learning and deepen knowledge through looking at specific aspects of houses and what they can learn from them.

Decisions about 'next step' teaching

Use evidence from the children's work to consider the next lesson on comparing the houses looked at in today's lesson with houses in specific historical times (e.g. Victorian).

Using ICT to contribute to the 'wider curriculum'

In this lesson the children are using ICT to enhance their communication skills. Depending on the availability of resources, the children could work in pairs. The pairs can be chosen so that those children with more advanced ICT skills support the less advanced. Some schools have set up 'mentoring partners' or 'learning buddies' for these types of situation.

Summary

- ICT can focus the lesson or series of lessons through the careful use of presentation software, OHTs or ICT-generated materials which can be used on a focused display.
- The World Wide Web or CD-ROMs can be very useful in finding secondary sources.
- Word-processing or DTP software is effective in helping children communicate their knowledge.
- Software can enable the work to be matched to differentiated needs through the support provided by such tools as word and picture banks.
- Children's work can be saved, printed, projected or displayed to form the focus for questions and answers, discussion, and to provide evidence of learning.
- Branching databases can be introduced to focus children's thinking on what you want them to learn.
- ICT can enhance the teaching and learning process, especially where there is a high level of resources.

Unit 5: How do we know about the Great Fire of London?

The children should have begun to learn about aspects of changes over time, aspects of the past and have had an introduction to people of the past through a unit on Florence Nightingale or other famous person.

Unless you are teaching near enough to London to visit the area where the Great Fire took place, your teaching will involve children learning through secondary sources. This learning will focus on specific aspects.

- Where did the fire take place?

- When did it take place?
- What were the main events and what were the consequences?
- Why did the fire occur?
- What evidence do we have about the Great Fire?

The QCA scheme of work for this unit can be found at **www.standards.dfes.gov.uk/schemes/history/his5?version=1**

Other sites are:

www.angliacampus.com/education/fire/london/history/ greatfir.htm (this link gives a picture, and a brief but useful description of the events)

www.bbc.co.uk/history/games/fire/index.shtml (this BBC site has an animation which shows the skyline before and after the fire; other information can be found from this site)

www.bbc.co.uk/history/timelines/britain/stu_greatfire.shtml (a timeline for the time of the Great Fire of London and related articles and information)

www.channel4.com/history/microsites/H/history/fire/ (this Channel 4 site has a number of links relating to the Great Fire: the story of the fire, an animation to show how the fire spread, a section called 'ask the experts', an examination of the legacy of the fire, a page of links to other related sites)

www.luminarium.org/encyclopedia/greatfire.htm (this site has a picture of the fire, information and a map)

www.schoolhistory.co.uk/primarylinks/fireofLondon.html (a number of articles giving information about the fire as well as links to other sites)

london.allinfo-about.com/features/pepysfire.html (a short piece of evidence based upon Samuel Pepy's diary)

www.nuffieldfoundation.org/primaryhistory/resources/ r_0028808.html (downloadable resources)

www.picturesofengland.com/london/map/firemap.html (a detailed map of London after the Great Fire)

Other sites can be found by making specific searches.

ICT opportunities

- Presentation software, word and picture banks, and the construction of worksheets have all been described before but they offer similar potential for supporting this unit. A section in the QCA scheme for this work lists the vocabulary that you might want to put into word banks as well as suggestions for resources.

- Pre-selected statements relating to the sequence of events for the Great Fire of London and also a series of pictures can be saved into word and picture banks. These can be saved in random order so the children have to place the statements, pictures or both into the correct sequence.

- The use of a Draw program will allow you to set up a timeline, which the children can complete. Children with more advanced ICT skills may be able to set up their own timeline. They can enter their own text in the relevant spaces, whilst others can use a word or picture bank to complete the timeline.

- Samuel Pepys, the famous diarist at the time of the Great Fire, is a good source of evidence. Showing children extracts from his diary from 2–6 September 1666 could be a starting point for children to write their own diary for those dates as an inhabitant of London at the time. You could ask them to choose a particular character involved in the Great Fire and write about their experiences.

- A fire can stimulate a great deal of interest and discussion whenever it takes place. Use Paint programs to allow the children to produce creative and imaginative images of the Great Fire.

- This unit offers opportunities to expand children's learning and links to other curriculum areas. Take the opportunity to discuss the dangers of fire. Make comparisons between the fire of 1666 and fires today, relating this to what they have learned about London at the time. The children could design posters to illustrate the dangers of fire using Paint, word-processing or DTP programs.

- Because the World Wide Web is such a huge resource, young children benefit from a structured approach – see the mountain trail in Chapter 2 as an example. You could also produce your own information sheet at the appropriate level.

- Software with speech facilities enables children to read and listen to text. You could write your own story about the Great Fire, which contains the facts and information you want the children to learn. Children could then be encouraged to write their own stories of the fire, or use the diaries suggested earlier. They could be shared with the whole class during the conclusion to a lesson, or series of lessons.

- ICT enables children to communicate through a range of media. It allows support to be given to the process of writing. The use of writing frames can guide the children to address specific questions. The use of a word bank can be supportive in helping children use the correct vocabulary. The example writing frame overleaf shows possible headings:

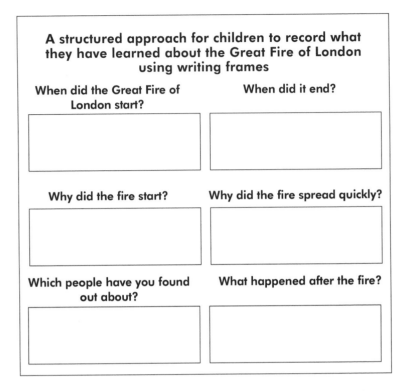

A structured approach for children to record what they have learned about the Great Fire of London using writing frames

When did the Great Fire of London start?

When did it end?

Why did the fire start?

Why did the fire spread quickly?

Which people have you found out about?

What happened after the fire?

Links to the QCA scheme of work for ICT
- Using a word bank (Unit 1B)
- The information around us (Unit 1C)
- Writing stories: communicating information using text (Unit 2A)
- Creating pictures (Unit 2B)
- Finding information (Unit 2C)
- Questions and answers (Unit 2E)
- Combining text and graphics (Unit 3A)
- Writing for different audiences (Unit 4A – this is a Year 4 unit in the QCA scheme, but the children's writing suggested here could be used as an introduction to the unit).

A LESSON PLAN: HOW DO WE KNOW ABOUT THE GREAT FIRE OF LONDON?

Title
How do we know about the Great Fire of London?

Year group
Year 2

Children's previous experience
- Know about things from the past through previous history lessons (e.g. toys, homes).
- Know about people and stories in history.
- Know how to use word-processing and/or DTP programs to input text and graphics.

Key questions or foci
- When was the Great Fire of London?
- Where did the Great Fire happen – in what city and what part of that city?
- What was the sequence of events?

History teaching objectives
- To learn the time and date of the Great Fire of London (2–6 September 1666).
- To learn that the fire happened in the City of London.
- To learn the sequence of events and why the fire started and ended.

ICT teaching objectives
- To read and listen to an electronic story about the fire in order to find out information.
- To use software programs to combine text and graphics to communicate what they have learned in the form of a diary, including the use of word and picture banks. (Some children may need more structure in the form of writing frames.)

Learning outcomes – assessment opportunities
- Children use ICT to integrate text and graphics into their writing about the fire. This can be in the form of a story, a diary or by using writing frames.
- Through this writing the children show they know the date and times of the fire, where it happened and the sequence of events.

Resources
For teachers: dependent on the resources available.
For children: software with word and picture banks, writing frames set up for the children to use.

Lesson sequence

Introduction
Introduce the unit and the lessons on the Great Fire of London. Use presentation software, data projector or interactive whiteboard (or other methods) to share the objectives, information and pictures to focus the lesson. Ask: what was the Great Fire of London? Where is London? When did it happen? What happened? Why did it happen?

Activities
Pre-prepare a story that the children can read and listen to at the computer. The children use the software to write their account of the Great Fire in the form of a diary or through the use of writing frames. Graphics can be accessed through a picture bank and a word bank will provide supporting vocabulary. Save the work to the children's folder when completed or if the lesson comes to an end and requires finishing at a later time. Support the children's use of software. Ensure the children know how to access the support materials. Monitor the learning as the children use the software. Depending on the resource level it may be necessary to have children work in pairs, or for some to work on the computer whilst others carry out related tasks away from the computer.

Conclusion
Review the children's learning through discussion and children's work. Make an assessment of how well the teaching objectives have been met. Project the children's work onto the whiteboard as a focus for discussion. Focus on the questions from the introduction.

Extension activities
Provide a resource with further links to information and pictures focusing on the reasons for the fire spreading so quickly.

Decisions about 'next step' teaching
Use the learning outcomes to identify those children who need further reinforcement of the teaching objectives for this lesson and those who can move to new learning. Identify those children who need further help with their use of ICT so that it is supportive rather than a barrier.

Using ICT to contribute to the 'wider curriculum'

The use of ICT can support the development of children's literacy. Carefully planned support within the software programs should enable children to succeed in communicating their learning at a level appropriate to them. Pairing children can help support both the history knowledge and the ICT skills necessary in this lesson.

Summary

- Using ICT in a context enables children to learn how to integrate text and graphics.
- Using word banks with appropriate vocabulary to the task supports children when using ICT to communicate.
- An e-story is a positive way in which children can access information. The use of text and speech enables children to work at levels appropriate to them. The less fluent reader can use the speech, whilst the more able reader can use both speech and text.
- Where data projectors and interactive whiteboards are available, children's work can be displayed for all the children to see. Children can talk about their work and share ideas.
- If the resources in your school are less developed, the use of CD, video and OHTs can all be used to enhance both the teaching and learning.

Unit 9: What was it like for children in the Second World War?

The QCA scheme for this unit can be found at **www.standards.dfes. gov.uk/schemes/history/his9?version=1**

Other sites that you might find useful can be found at:

www.iwm.org.uk/education/lifeinww2/ (this site is provided by the Imperial War Museum and provides information to support enquiry and research)

learningcurve.pro.gov.uk/snapshots/snapshot09/ snapshot9.htm (this site has a number of posters from the Second World War which can be enlarged or copied and used to answer a range of questions, or be the focus for children's tasks; a section of related web links are included as well as links to the QCA scheme of work and the National Curriculum).

The teacher and ICT

The Second World War is outside the experience of the children but they can learn through a range of media as well as through the first-hand experience of relatives, friends or other adults invited into school. In this unit you could consider using ICT resources not mentioned before. The use of a video camera to record an interview with a Second World War veteran means that the interview can be revisited.

Finding suitable resources such as maps, pictures, posters and websites can be time-consuming but you will benefit by building up a bank of resources that can be used as the unit progresses, or with future classes. Saved resource banks in ICT can easily be added to, edited and changed to make them relevant and appropriate to different children.

This unit focuses on the effect of the war on children. This will involve selecting information about the following.

- What was meant by evacuation?
- Where were the children evacuated from and to?
- What happened to evacuee children?
- How did the children feel about being away from their parents?

ICT opportunities
The following aspects of using ICT have already been identified in different contexts and would be applicable when teaching this unit.

- Use presentation software in conjunction with data projectors and interactive whiteboards to allow children to see:
  - maps as a point of discussion relating to which countries were involved in the war (cross-curricular links to geography)
  - pictures of clothes that were worn at the time
  - war posters as a focus for discussion
  - pictures of leaders of countries involved in the war
  - pictures of the Blitz
  - pictures and lists of typical foods at the time of the war and what rationing meant in terms of a typical meal
  - a series of slides to focus on the main teaching points for the lesson, series of lessons or even the unit.
- Use word-processing or DTP software to enable children to write a diary as if they were children in the war. They will need to find out information about aspects of the war, including food rationing and evacuees. Children could consider what it might feel like to be away from parents for a long period of time.
- Ask the children to think about being an evacuee and writing to their parents about their feelings and experiences. Children's writing provides evidence of how well they have understood what it was like to be a child in the war and to go through these experiences.
- If possible, set up e-mail links to people who were children during the war. Using e-mail in this way could help the children gain some understanding about what it was like to be a child at that time. As the children progress through the unit they may come up with questions which would be best answered by someone with first-hand experience.
- Bring examples of newspapers from the war into the classroom or view them on the web. DTP programs help children to create their own newspapers and learn about using columns, different fonts for headlines and highlighting specific points. They also allow pictures to be imported.
- Present pictures of aspects from the war to the children and ask them to add captions and short pieces of text to illustrate what they have learned from the picture. Ask specific questions to guide children to use the evidence to make inferences or draw conclusions.

- E-stories are another way in which children can communicate. You could provide different situations and contexts for the story. Using the appropriate software and the tools enable children to put in text and link the pages. Original stories can be shared with the class or used by other children. Speech facilities in some programs allow children to listen to the story. As children progress in their use of ICT, voice, sound, music and animations can be added to enhance their work.
- Use cameras and video to enhance your teaching and make the war 'come alive'. Digital and video cameras can be used to take photographs of artefacts as well as to record interviews. Video can be played back to remind children of what was said.
- A web trail could guide children to particular sites or files where they can find information to answer specific questions. Links to video clips, sound files and pictures could also be included.

Links to the QCA scheme of work for ICT
- Using a word bank (Unit 1B)
- The information around us (Unit 1C)
- Writing stories: communicating information through text (Unit 2A)
- Creating pictures (Unit 2B)
- Finding information (Unit 2C)
- Questions and answers (Unit 2E)
- Combining text and graphics (Unit 3A)
- Manipulating sound (Unit 3B)
- E-mail (Unit 3E)
- Writing for different audiences (Unit 4A)
- Collecting and presenting information: questionnaires and pie charts (Unit 4D).

Other units from the scheme that are identified as being taught after Years 3 and 4 might support your work depending on the skill level of the children and the resources available. These are as follows.

- Evaluating information, checking accuracy and questioning plausibility (Unit 5C)
- Multimedia presentation (Unit 6A)
- Using the Internet to search large databases and to interpret information (Unit 6D).

A LESSON PLAN: WHAT WAS IT LIKE FOR CHILDREN IN THE SECOND WORLD WAR?

Title
What was it like for children in Second World War?

Year group
Years 3–4

Children's previous experience
- Knowledge of different times, how people used to live and the houses they lived in.

- Know how to find information and other resources through secondary sources, including the use of ICT.

Key questions or foci
- Why were children evacuated?
- Where were children evacuated from and to?
- How did children feel about being away from their parents?

History teaching objectives
- To understand why children were evacuated.
- To understand what evacuees felt about their situation and to empathise with them.

ICT teaching objectives
- To use a word-processing program to compose a letter.
- To access a word bank to support their writing.
- To access information sources to support their writing.

Learning outcomes – assessment opportunities
- Children are able to compose a letter to their parents, which shows they have some understanding of what it was like to be a child evacuee. (It is unlikely that this lesson would be the first one you teach in this unit and the letter writing would need to develop from previous teaching.)

Resources
For teachers: data projector, interactive whiteboard, presentation software.
For children: word-processing or DTP software with word bank and picture bank facility.

Lesson sequence

Introduction
Lead a whole-class introduction to this lesson using presentation software, data projector or interactive whiteboard, OHP or display.

Activities
See ICT opportunities (pages 45–46).

Conclusion
Review the children's learning through discussion and children's work. Make an assessment of how well the teaching objectives have been met. Project the children's work onto the whiteboard as a focus for discussion.

Using ICT to contribute to the 'wider curriculum'
This lesson can contribute effectively to aspects of the 'wider curriculum' since it is necessary for the children to gain knowledge and understanding of the evacuee before they are able to place themselves in that situation in order to write the letter home. In the context of this lesson it is possible to identify aspects of spiritual, moral, social and cultural development as well as citizenship, some aspects of the key skills and thinking skills.

Summary
- ICT is an excellent source of materials to help children learn about the Second World War. Access to maps, pictures, animations, video and sound clips and information in the form of text can all support the learning.
- The use of tape recorders, digital and video cameras can be used to record interviews.
- Word-processing and DTP software programs enable children to write and communicate what they have learned in a variety of forms: letters, diaries, newspaper articles and picture captions. The programs allow for drafting and redrafting as well as the use of word and picture banks and spell and grammar checks. The use of different fonts can be used to

highlight particular parts of the text.

- E-mail can be used to write to people about their war experiences. This is especially useful when those people cannot get into school. It is also possible, with their agreement, to get these people to respond to specific questions as the work progresses.
- Pre-prepared e-stories, or ones written by the children, can provide interest, enjoyment and a new way of learning about children in the war.
- CD-ROMs can also be used a source of information and pictures, tell stories of the war which support your objectives and, in some cases, enable children to role play or carry out simulations.

Unit 13: How has life changed in Britain since 1948?

In this unit there are several areas that could be investigated to help the children.

- Materials – containers, the development of plastic and changes in clothes.
- The development of electrical goods in the home.
- The recent development of computers.
- Changes in various types of transport.
- Changes in population.

The children could be asked for other areas that they consider would show how things have changed. You would expect that by Years 5 and 6 the children would:

- be able to compare the present to aspects of the past and draw conclusions;
- know how people lived in the past and what similarities and differences there are between those times and today;
- know about famous people through history and their influence on events that have taken place;
- know that history is about finding evidence and be able to question that evidence;
- be able to extract evidence on the basis of information sources.

The QCA site for this unit can be found at **www.standards.dfee. gov.uk/schemes/history/his13?version=1**

Other useful sites are:

www.eadt.co.uk/eduzone/Cars/content/asp/natcurric.asp (has cars since 1930s divided into decades and associated information from newspapers relating to different aspects of history since 1948)

www.schoolhistory.co.uk/primarylinks/britainsince1930.html (this site has a number of links to relevant information for this unit)

www.4learning.co.uk/essentials/history/units/ postwar_bi.shtml (a range of sources of information with both pictures and text).

The teacher and ICT

This unit covers a time span of 50 years so there are many changes that you might want to focus upon. The use of artefacts helps children gain first-hand experience but they may not be available. A combination of whole-class introductions and group activities can widen the scope of the learning.

Whichever organisation you choose, ICT can be used to support your teaching and the children's learning. Access to information and support materials can be gained from the education site of the Public Records Office at **www.pro.gov.uk/education/default.htm** The census for 2001 is available at **www.statistics.gov.uk/census2001/default.asp** This site could be used to find information about the population and other changes. Both of the above sites could help you plan your teaching and prepare materials for the children to use.

You will need to evaluate any information you want the children to use for its validity and level. Specific Internet searches could provide video clips or speeches by famous people that relate to particular historical events over this time period. This unit lends itself well to children being involved in historical research and enquiry.

ICT opportunities

- When preparing presentation software to introduce a lesson you might want to link to a specific web page. This can be done through linking to the Internet, but it may take time for the page to open. One way to avoid a slow connection is to download the page and make a link to it from one of your slides. Links to other files and pictures on your computer can also make your presentation more immediate. This allows you to select the focus through text, pictures, sound and video. Schools with broadband connections have the advantage of increased speed when accessing websites.

- Set up a time trail to help children find information from specific websites (as suggested in other sections). A worksheet or question and answer page could follow a similar format. Add word banks of appropriate vocabulary and pictures to support children in answering the questions or when you ask them to carry out written work. Some sites already have links to other sites and these can be a useful access point for children. Alternatively, the children can use Favourites or Bookmarks to save favourite sites.

- Databases can be a source of information, or they can be set up to collect information, which can then be interrogated. The children could organise their pictures of artefacts into groups under a number of headings such as the decade in which they were made. The data collections can also be used to produce graphs.

- Produce spreadsheets to compare different aspects of different decades. Children might find information about the costs of different appliances over the 50 years and produce a graph to identify the changes in cost.

Links to the QCA scheme of work for ICT

- Introduction to databases (Unit 3C)
- Exploring simulations (Unit 3D)
- Writing for different audiences (Unit 4A)
- Collecting and presenting information: questionnaires and pie charts (Unit 4D)
- Analysing data and asking questions using complex searches (Unit 5B)
- Evaluating information, checking accuracy and questioning plausibility (Unit 5C)
- Introduction to spreadsheets (Unit 5D)
- Multimedia presentation (Unit 6A)
- Spreadsheet modelling (Unit 6B)
- Using the Internet to search large databases and to interpret information (Unit 6D).

A LESSON PLAN: HOW HAS LIFE IN BRITAIN CHANGED SINCE 1948?

The focus for this lesson or series of lessons is population changes between 1948 and 2001. One lesson may not be enough time to gather the information in order for the children to draw conclusions.

Title
How has life in Britain changed since 1948?

Year group
Year 5/6

Children's previous experience
- Know about changes over time and what things are the same and what are different
- Can access historical information and answer questions based upon it.
- Have learned about people of the past.
- Can communicate their knowledge and understanding of history in a variety of ways, including the use of ICT.

Key questions or foci
- How have the populations of major cities changed over the last 50 years?
- What is the explanation for these changes?

History teaching objectives
- To know that populations of the UK's major cities have changed between 1948 and 2001.
- To explain why those changes have occurred.

ICT teaching objectives
- To know how to find information about population.
- To collect the information.
- To use a spreadsheet to input data collected and produce appropriate graphical representation of the data.

Learning outcomes – assessment opportunities
- The children use spreadsheets to produce graphs of the changes in population of the UK's major cities.

- They use the census and other information provided to explain why these changes have taken place.
- They use DTP or presentation software to communicate their findings.

Resources
For teachers: data projector, interactive whiteboard, presentation software.
For children: access to information sources (e.g. Internet), spreadsheet software.

Lesson sequence

Introduction
Introduce the lesson, or series of lessons, on populations changes 1948–2001. Use presentation software, data projector or interactive whiteboard (or other methods) to share the objectives, information and pictures to focus the lesson.

Activities
Children use methods of enquiry to locate information about the population change in major cities over the last 50 years (electronic worksheet, Internet search, pre-bookmarked sites, and so on). A hyperlink to the census or other sites enables the children to have immediate access to the information you want them to use. The census site requires navigation and it would not be desirable to simply download one page in this instance. If your school does not have the resources to allow all the children to access the census site at the same time, you need to consider the most effective organisation. In some cases you may prefer to print out the relevant information and the children find the information away from the computer. This could be done in pairs or groups. Children use spreadsheet software to input data and create graphical representation. (You may find that you have to prepare for the children's use of spreadsheets by direct teaching prior to this lesson. The provision of a data projector and interactive whiteboard can involve the children.) They use key questions to interrogate the data and explain why these changes have taken place.

Conclusion
Review the children's learning through discussion and their work. Make an assessment of how well the teaching objectives have been met. Project the children's work onto the whiteboard as a focus for discussion.

Summary
- Children in Year 6 should have an understanding of the historical concepts, be able to build on previous teaching and learning and use a variety of tools to communicate what they have found out.
- You need to be aware of the ICT skills, knowledge and understanding of the children to make the use of spreadsheets possible.
- The use of spreadsheets to collect and display data can help the children analyse data and come to conclusions.
- The use of one source of information can help the children think why this evidence is plausible and valid.
- ICT can support a variety of ways for children to communicate their ideas and learning.

Conclusion

This chapter has covered four units for the QCA history scheme of work and suggested ways in which you might choose to use ICT as a support for teaching and learning. The way you choose to use ICT yourself or with the children will have to be guided by the range of both hardware and software, and by decisions regarding its appropriate use.

Preparation is key to your success in the classroom and you should make sure that the use of ICT does not mask the history you want the children to learn. As the children progress, the potential uses of ICT will require the children to develop skills in both the use of software and hardware. If the ICT skills are not taught and developed, the children are likely to lose focus on the history objectives.

4 Using ICT to support teaching and learning in primary RE

This chapter focuses on using ICT to support teaching and learning in RE in primary schools. RE is a legal requirement, but unlike other subjects RE content is delivered in accordance with the locally agreed syllabus. See **www.nc.uk.net/servlets/Subjects?Subject=Re** for links to:

- non-statutory guidance;
- schemes of work from the QCA;
- model syllabuses;
- a glossary of terms;
- the Virtual Teachers' Centre for supporting resources.

The National Curriculum site and the associated links are a useful resource to identify the legal requirements in respect of teaching and learning RE in primary schools. BECTa also provides information about the entitlement to ICT in RE at **www.ictadvice.org.uk/ index.php?section=tl&rid=2435&wn=1** The following headings are taken from this site and are what you would expect to find in the agreed syllabus where you teach.

- *What people believe;*
- *How people put their beliefs into practice;*
- *How people express their beliefs;*
- *Similarities and differences in and between religions;*
- *The influence of religion on individuals, communities and society;*
- *The cultural context of religions;*

and to learn from religion by fostering:

- *awareness of own beliefs, values and commitments;*
- *reflection on experience, meaning and purpose;*
- *evaluating religious responses to life;*
- *respect for others;*
- *handling uncertainty, ambiguity and controversy.*

As can be seen from these headings, RE has a very wide scope and is not only about knowledge and understanding of different religions but also 'learning from' them and how they might impact on their lives and the lives of others. These two aspects and other supporting materials can be found in the QCA model syllabuses for RE at **www.qca.org.uk/ca/subjects/re/model_syllabus.asp**

RE and ICT

Learning about religions: Attainment Target 1

In helping children to gain knowledge and understanding about religions, ICT can play a significant part. The use of the Internet and CD-ROMs give access to a wide range of information as well as pictures, video and sound clips, which can form the basis for discussion and help develop an understanding of religious beliefs and practices. Children can access holy texts, pictures and art and graphics associated with a range of religions being studied. The careful selection and use of information enables comparisons to be drawn and the identification of similarities and differences. Electronic communication enables the teacher and the children to connect with 'experts' who can be asked questions about their religion and form a basis for 'informed' learning. By learning 'about' different religions children should understand that within one religion there may be diverse traditions and beliefs such as those evidenced in Christianity. ICT can help both teachers and children to 'learn about' religion by giving:

- access to information that develops knowledge and under-standing and enhances the children's investigative and enquiry skills;
- access to a wide range of sources where the validity and plausibility can be questioned;
- information through pictures, video and sound, which supports knowledge and understanding;
- a variety of means to organise, record, report and commu-nicate the knowledge and understanding they have gained;
- the opportunity to link with people who can help develop knowledge and understanding;
- the ability to record pictures and sounds of people who can tell the children about different faiths.

Learning from religions: Attainment Target 2

This aspect of RE may be considered harder to access and will depend upon the age and abilities of the children. In the model syllabus this is called Attainment Target 2 and includes the ability to:

- *give an informed and considered response to religious and moral issues;*
- *reflect on what might be learnt from religions in the light of one's own beliefs and experiences;*
- *identify and respond to questions of meaning within religions.*

ICT can provide information and background knowledge that would enable the children to engage in these issues in a meaningful and purposeful way. Children can be asked to respond to specific scenarios about religious or moral issues through writing using ICT. ICT can be the vehicle for children to communicate their own beliefs and experiences, and give personal accounts which can be shared with others in the class. ICT can also be the tool through which questions are generated and asked, as well as a way in which responses are gathered and shared.

ICT is particularly useful to help children to learn about religions when first-hand experience may not be immediately available. As with the subjects covered in previous chapters this will involve you in careful planning and preparation but the benefits will be in the development of the children's knowledge and understanding. As an example, 'virtual' tours of religious buildings can be accessed using ICT to support teaching and learning. Two such sites are **www.hitchams.suffolk.sch.uk/synagogue/** and **www.vryork.com/minster/minster_index.html**

For teachers ICT can:

- enhance and support subject knowledge and expertise;
- enable the teaching to be more stimulating for the children;
- facilitate links and contacts with RE subject specialists and experts.

To show how ICT can be used in RE, this chapter looks at four units selected from the QCA scheme of work for RE. They span both key stages and look at a range of content.

- What is the Torah and why is it important to Jewish people? (Unit 2A, Year 2)
- How and why do Hindus celebrate Divali? (Unit 3B, Year 3)
- Why is Muhammad important to Muslims? (Unit 5A, Year 5)
- What can we learn from Christian religious buildings? (Unit 6E, Year 6).

Unit 2A: *What is the Torah and why is it important to Jewish people?*

The link for the QCA scheme of work for this unit can be found at **www.standards.dfes.gov.uk/schemes/religion/ rel2a?version=1**

Other useful sites in supporting this unit can be found at:

www.educate.org.uk/teacher_zone/classroom/re/unit2a.htm (gives example lesson plans, worksheets and links to other sites)

www.icteachers.co.uk/resources/re/torah_laws.doc (a source of information about the Torah and its contents, which are set out under headings)

atschool.eduweb.co.uk/carolrb/judaism/artefa.html (information about artefacts relating to the Jewish faith alongside pictures).

Further sites and resources can be accessed through using search engines or by links from the QCA Standards site and the BECTa site.

The teacher and ICT

The knowledge base necessary to plan, prepare and deliver lessons is crucial. In the QCA scheme the following headings are given as objectives.

- What is the Torah?
- How can books teach us how to live?
- Making a Torah scroll
- Preparing a visit to a synagogue
- Visit to a synagogue
- What have we learnt about the Torah?

This unit allows for a combination of direct teaching, investigation by the children, the use of secondary sources and visits to learn through first-hand experience. As an introduction you will need to prepare materials that help children learn about the Jews and the Torah and what this means to the Jewish people. The main ideas you need to teach are as follows.

- The Torah is made up of the first five books of the Bible.
- The Torah is handwritten.
- It is written in Hebrew and kept in an ark at the synagogue.
- The vocabulary to describe the important parts of the synagogue and the artefacts that have special meaning to the Jews.
- What are the Holiness code and the Ten Commandments?
- What are mitzvoth?

For some of the above items you could ask the children to use information sources with the help of focused questions and structured guidance.

The use of data projectors in conjunction with interactive whiteboards is extremely helpful in sharing information and teaching objectives with the children. If your school has a lower level of resources, alternative methods such as the use of an OHP or stand-alone computer may be used. If you have a computer suite then pre-prepared materials can be saved to the school server so that children can access them. If this is your situation then you will have to think carefully about teaching strategies that make best use of the available resources.

ICT opportunities

- This unit involves a range of vocabulary that may not be familiar to the children. Prepare a word bank to help the children write about the Torah and its importance to Jewish people.
- Similarly, create a picture bank so that children can link pictures and descriptions. Pictures and words can be accessed and placed onto the writing page. The children can add their own explanations so that there is a degree of independent learning. You can download pictures from specific websites or

take them with a digital camera during a visit to a synagogue. A visiting Rabbi could be asked to bring relevant artefacts. Pictures can be viewed on the computer or could be printed out for use in a class display.

- At this age you would not expect children to be able to use video with computers but you could take video footage and play it back during a lesson, or install it onto the computers for children to view. This would be a useful support if you were unable to arrange a visit to a synagogue as it lets the children see aspects of the Jewish religion that may not be available first-hand.

- Children can present their work in a variety of ways away from the computer (writing, painting, drawing, speech), but the use of technology means children can use Draw or Paint programs to create their own representation of the Torah and associated items.

- The use of presentation software, word-processing or DTP programs are all ways in which children can present their work. Such work can be shared on a network or printed out to be used as part of a focused display.

- The combination of information gathered from the World Wide Web and CD-ROMs can help you focus the children on what you want them to learn. The use of the interactive whiteboard can involve the children and is a helpful resource for you to plan and present relevant information.

- Where it is possible, and available, e-mail communication with a Rabbi or other 'expert' can aid children's learning through asking questions and receiving replies. If the children are unable to use e-mail you can collate their questions and send them as one message. The reply can be used to further enhance learning.

Links to the QCA scheme of work for ICT

- Using a word bank (Unit 1B)
- The information around us (Unit 1C)
- Labelling and classifying (Unit 1D)
- Writing stories: communicating information using text (Unit 2A)
- Creating pictures (Unit 2B)
- Finding information (Unit 2C)
- Questions and answers (Unit 2E).

A LESSON PLAN: WHAT IS THE TORAH AND WHY IS IT IMPORTANT TO JEWISH PEOPLE?

This lesson plan is an introduction to the Torah before developing other aspects of this unit.

Title
What is the Torah?

Year group
Year 2

Key questions or foci
- What is the Torah? In which religion is the Torah important? Why is it important to Jewish people?

RE teaching objectives
- **AT1:** To learn about the Torah and why it is special to the Jews.
- **AT2:** To learn about what is valuable to them and relate this to their learning about the Torah.

ICT teaching objectives
- To access pictures and vocabulary from word banks and integrate them into their writing on the computer

Learning outcomes – assessment opportunities
- **AT1:** The children are able to explain describe the Torah and why it is important to the Jews.
- **AT2:** The children are able to select and identify things that are of value to themselves and say why, and link this to the Torah.
- **ICT:** Children show they can communicate effectively about the Torah using a word-processing or DTP program and integrate words and pictures from word banks.

Resources
For teachers: presentation software, data projector or interactive whiteboard (or OHP and acetates).
For children: word-processing or DTP software, word and picture banks.

Lesson sequence

Introduction
Use presentation software to show the children pictures and text taken from the Torah in order to focus the discussion, raise questions and share the objectives with the children. If you have a low level of ICT resources, use an OHP to display pictures and text. Reinforce the skills required to carry out the task.

Activities
See ICT opportunities (pages 56–57).

Conclusion
Save the children's work to disk and share it with the whole class using the data projector and interactive whiteboard. Encourage the children to talk about their work. Where there are lower levels of resources add the children's work to a display where ICT has been used to produce banners, text and pictures. Add focused questions in clear, bold type.

Using ICT to contribute to the 'wider curriculum'
Using ICT in this context enables children to learn and know about the Jewish faith and what aspects are important to them. In learning about the Torah, children can begin to understand how it guides the lives of Jewish people. The use of ICT can enable children to find out information that may not be available by other means. Their knowledge can be related to social, cultural, moral and spiritual aspects of their own lives.

ICT can also contribute to:
- the setting of suitable learning challenges through differentiated tastes;
- responding to children's diverse learning needs by enabling them to access information in a variety of ways;
- overcoming barriers to learning and assessment by using a variety of applications and tools;
- developing language across the curriculum by the use of subject-specific vocabulary banks.

Summary
- ICT is able to support learning in this unit by bringing information to the children if they are

unable to access it through first-hand experience.
- Word and picture banks can support the learning by making material accessible in electronic form.
- Video taken by the teacher can make the teaching focused and be a useful source of secondary information.

Unit 3B: How and why do Hindus celebrate Divali?

This unit introduces children to the Hindu religion through their festival of Divali. (Divali is also celebrated by Sikhs.) It is a celebration time seen through a number of aspects:

- a festival of light;
- storytelling about good and evil through the story of Rama and Sita;
- the use of oil lamps called divas;
- various religious symbols;
- greeting cards, photos and posters;
- rangoli patterns.

Depending on where you teach, you may be able to call upon Hindus or Sikhs to talk about Divali and other aspects of their religion. If you have Hindu children in your class they may also be able to contribute or be willing to bring in artefacts for the class to look at and talk about. If first-hand experiences are not available you will have to look for other ways to help the children learn. The link to the QCA scheme of work for this unit is at **www.standards.dfes.gov.uk/schemes/religion/rel3b?version=1**

Websites that you can use to support this unit can be found at:

www.re.leonet.co.uk/agreedsyllabus/y3diwali.html (an example of a local plan, which you will find in whatever LEA you teach)

www.educate.org.uk/teacher_zone/classroom/re/unit3b.htm (some suggestions for teaching and some useful links that both you and the children could use)

www.calcuttayellowpages.com/diwali.html (a full explanation of what Divali is and how Hindus celebrate this time of the year)

www.clickwalla.com/article.php?cid=86&aid=864 (background information).

All these sites have background information and graphics that can be copied and downloaded. You can also use a search engine to explore further sites for supporting this unit.

The teacher and ICT
Before teaching this unit you will need a personal knowledge base. The children may have different perspectives depending on their personal beliefs and backgrounds. The Hindu child will have taken

part in Divali celebrations and be aware of what happens, the associated stories and other aspects of the celebrations. Children not of the Hindu faith may not have this knowledge and you will have to look for other sources of information.

Preparation of background information using ICT can be the same for most situations. If you teach in a school with Hindu children you could involve them in sharing their own experiences if you feel it will not embarrass them or make them uncomfortable. Where the children are not aware of the Hindu religion and the meaning of Divali you will have to be explicit in your use of information and explanations. ICT can engage the children in activities which help them learn.

ICT opportunities

- Build a word bank that relates to the festival of Divali – for example, Hindu, Hinduism, Lakshmi, diva, rangoli, moral, shrine. Add to the word bank as you or the children find more words that are specific to the religion or the festival.
- Build a picture bank relating to Divali. Include Hindu gods and goddesses, Lakshmi, pictures of Rama and Sita and other characters from the story, pictures of rangoli patterns, symbols relating to Hinduism and Divali, examples of greetings cards sent at the time of Divali. A bank of pictures such as this can be used to support the children's knowledge, used in their writing, or as a guide to answering specific questions.
- The story of Rama and Sita is central to Divali as a story of good overcoming evil. Children can have access to this story through the use of ICT. It can also be shared with the whole class where you have projection facilities. The children can learn how to make e-stories on a similar theme so they can be shared with others in the class. Use DTP software to enable the children to retell the story themselves with pictures added from the picture bank. Children with more advanced ICT skills could be guided to specific sites where they can choose pictures they think suitable to enhance their writing. These sites can be saved to their Favourites or Bookmarks for ease of access in the future. Use presentation software to enable the children to tell the story and insert pictures.
- You may need to differentiate the work by structuring how the children tell the story. The example above would be for those children who have confidence in typing onto the computer and inserting pictures. Pre-prepared pictures and word banks with text can be moved and sequenced so that the story is in the correct order. It is also possible to set up a 'storyboard' approach where a number of text boxes are pre-prepared for the children to sequence the story and add text and pictures. Children could prepare their own storyboard or comic strip story based upon the idea of good overcoming evil.

- If you can establish links with someone outside the school who is willing for the children to email questions then, as in previous sections, this becomes a highly relevant source of information to children as they work.
- Encourage the children to use DTP software in a variety of ways. They may design and write their own Divali card, draw pictures of divas and explain what they are, design their own rangoli pattern or write about characters in the stories. Once again, this writing could be imaginative and individual, or more structured where writing skills, ICT skills (or both) need support.

Links to the QCA scheme of work for ICT

- Using a word bank (Unit 1B)
- The information around us (Unit 1C)
- Writing stories: communicating information through text (Unit 2A)
- Creating pictures (Unit 2B)
- Finding information (Unit 2C)
- Questions and answers (Unit 2E)
- Combining text and graphics (Unit 3A)
- E-mail (Unit 3E)
- Writing for different audiences (Unit 4A)
- Developing images using repeating patterns (Unit 4B).

A LESSON PLAN: HOW AND WHY DO HINDUS CELEBRATE DIVALI?

Title
The story of Rama and Sita

Year group
Year 3

Key questions or foci
- Who were Rama and Sita? What was their story about? What can we learn from them in our lives?

RE teaching objectives
AT1: To learn about the story of Rama and Sita and its importance in the tradition of Hindus.
AT2:. To learn how the story of Rama and Sita shows how good can overcome evil and relate it to their own lives.

ICT teaching objectives
- To learn how to compose an e-story using the link tool in word-processing or DTP software.

Learning outcomes – assessment opportunities
- **AT1:** Children show they know the story of Rama and Sita and why it is important in the Hindu religion.
- **AT2:** By writing a story where good overcomes evil the children show they understand the moral of the story.
- **ICT:** Children use word-processing or DTP software to compose an e-story where pages are linked together through graphics or text.

Resources

For teachers: presentation software, data projector or interactive whiteboard (or OHP and acetates).
For children: DTP software, word and picture banks.

Lesson sequence

Introduction

Introduce the lesson with projected pictures of Rama and Sita and use presentation software to show the story in the form of a storyboard. Alternatively, project story pictures on an OHP or use a big book.

Activities

See ICT opportunities (pages 60–61).

Conclusion

Project the children's stories onto an interactive whiteboard and invite the children to show and tell their story. If there is a lower level of resourcing, save the stories to computer and ask the children to read and listen to them at a later date. If the children have produced their stories but the facilities do not allow them to be shared they can be printed out and displayed to be read as hard copy.

Using ICT to contribute to the 'wider curriculum'

The story can be used to develop children's thinking, oral and literacy skills. The use of Rama and Sita as a way into thinking about opposites and can link into areas of citizenship.

Summary

- The use of ICT in this context can support children's learning about a faith of which they may not have first-hand experience.
- ICT enables children to record and communicate what they have learned.
- ICT tools allow access to 'experts' as a secondary source of information.

Unit 5A: Why is Muhammad important to Muslims?

This unit builds on others the children will have followed in previous years. In learning about Muhammad (PBUH) the children can think about work they have done relating to other faiths and how they found out about the main points. The letters after Muhammad's name denote respect and mean 'Praise be unto Him'.

In this unit the focus is on the following aspects.

- How Muhammad's life was changed.
- The Qur'an as the holy book of the Muslims.
- How Muslims learn the teachings of the Qur'an, and what they teach.
- The Qur'an does not allow pictures of Allah, Muhammad, the prophets, any person or animal.
- The five pillars of Islam.
- Important festivals in the Muslim calendar (Ramadan, Eid-Ul-Fitr).
- Mecca and its importance.

A primary resource would be to invite adult Muslims in your school or local community to talk about their faith, beliefs and traditions.

The link to the QCA scheme for this unit can be found at **www.standards.dfes.gov.uk/schemes/religion/ rel5a?version=1**

Other supporting websites are:

www.educate.org.uk/teacher_zone/classroom/re/unit5a.htm (supporting information in the form of fact files, lesson plans, worksheets and links to other appropriate sites)

www.frenchwood.co.uk/festival.htm (a primary school site with information and graphics to help you plan this unit)

atschool.eduweb.co.uk/carolrb/islam/islamintro.html (a range of information about Muslims, Muhammad and the Muslim way of life).

It is important to remember that, for many Muslims, pictures of people or animals are not acceptable. Bear this in mind when you are preparing to introduce the unit or when making a display. There is, however, an opportunity for work on patterns and design.

The teacher and ICT

When introducing a new topic such as this it is important to engage the children. You may decide to think about common themes that link into how Muhammad's life changed and the consequences of that event. Sharing the story of Muhammad and other similar stories with the whole class using projected images can be both effective and motivating. If the children have the capability they can be encouraged to read the stories to the rest of the class or individuals can read different parts. This can lead to discussion about how Muhammad might have felt or how people who knew Muhammad might have reacted to his story. These could be linked to other stories where people have had life-changing experiences.

As this is a Year 5 unit you would expect the children to be more independent learners but a structured learning environment helps children find relevant and appropriate information. For those children who are more confident in using ICT tools, Internet searches would allow an 'open-ended' approach to be adopted.

The vocabulary may be new to some children and so the setting up of a word bank would be extremely useful for both the children and as a guide to direct teaching. Research into Muhammad and the Muslim faith is crucial if you are to help the children learn about, and from, a faith with which they may not be familiar. Provision of appropriate ICT applications enables children to show evidence of their learning.

ICT opportunities

- ICT involves more than the use of computers although many of the ideas presented in this book have focused on this aspect of ICT. The use of presentation software and projected images has been identified in other sections but introducing a unit or lesson about Muhammad can involve the use of video, CD-ROM or sound recordings. All of these can identify the objectives, introduce the children to their tasks, and give them information that leads into their own work.

- Many Muslims do not have pictures of Muhammad or other human figures – their art is based upon design. Children can research the different designs and use a Paint or Draw program to produce their own. Use software to enable the children to include text that relates their work to that of Muslim art.
- The story of Muhammad is very special to Muslim people. Children can read the story and retell it from a different perspective. This retelling can fit into your work in the Literacy Strategy and helps the children use their literacy skills in a specific context. The use of ICT also enables children to draft and redraft their work and use word banks to include appropriate and specific vocabulary.
- As the children move towards Years 5 and 6 a degree of independent learning should be encouraged. This needs to be structured in way that helps the children learn in a managed environment. Using the link facility in many word-processing programs enables you to set up a series of questions that focuses learning or may be used for assessment purposes. The link can be made to other files or to the internet so that children can research or investigate questions. Clicking on a word or picture can link to a page giving an immediate response to their answer.

> **What is the name of the Muslims' special book?**
> Click on the one the answer you think is correct.
> Is it:
> a) the Bible?
> b) the Qur'an?
> c) the Torah?
>
> In this case the correct word is linked to a page that says WELL DONE and moves the child on, whilst the wrong answer links to a page that says TRY AGAIN and takes the child back to the question.
>
> Using ICT in this way can help the children learn as well as reinforcing their knowledge. The use of links to give feedback is a helpful tool and can support independent learning.

- By Year 5 you would expect the children's ICT skills to be such that they could use presentation software to produce an effective method of communicating to the rest of the class, or to other classes. This can include text, graphics, and links to sound and perhaps video if it is available. Where projection facilities are available they can talk through aspects of their work. This can help them consider how to present to different audiences. Presentation software allows children to exhibit their ICT skills, knowledge and understanding as well as showing their level of understanding of the topic being taught.

Links to the QCA scheme of work for ICT

Several of those units identified previously would be appropriate, and could be used to support this unit. Specific units are as follows:

- Writing for different audiences (Unit 4A)
- Developing images using repeating patterns (Unit 4B)
- Evaluating information, checking accuracy and questioning plausibility (Unit 5C)
- Multimedia presentation (Unit 6A)
- Using the Internet to search large databases and interpret information (Unit 6D).

A LESSON PLAN: WHY IS MUHAMMAD IMPORTANT TO MUSLIMS?

Title
Muhammad (PBUH) in his historical and geographical context.

Year group
Year 5

Key questions or foci
Who was Muhammad? When did he live? Why is he important to Muslims?

RE teaching objectives
AT1: To learn about Muhammad in his historical and geographical context.
AT2: To learn why Muhammad is important to Muslims and how his life affects how Muslims live.

ICT teaching objectives
- To employ research and enquiry skills when using the internet and CD-ROMs to find out about the life of Muhammad.

Learning outcomes – assessment opportunities
- **AT1:** For children to show evidence that they know who Muhammad was and when and where he lived.
- **AT2:** For children to show an understanding of the impact events in Muhammad's life have had on the followers of Islam and relate these to their own lives.
- **ICT:** For children to communicate their findings using ICT applications and tools appropriate to their ICT skill level.
- To show they can communicate the results of their research in an appropriate way.

Resources
For teachers: presentation software, data projector, interactive whiteboard (or OHP and acetates, video player).
For children: computer suite, Internet access, CD-ROMs.

Lesson sequence

Introduction
Use presentation software and an interactive whiteboard or data projector to introduce the lesson. Alternatively, use an OHP or video player to give information about Muhammad. Where computers are available in the classroom pre-prepared information could be loaded onto the computer to support children's work where facilities do not allow whole-class activities.

Activities
See ICT opportunities (pages 63–64).

Conclusion

Project the children's work as a focus for questions and discussion on what they have learned. Print out work and display it, or save it onto the classroom computers for other children to access. The work can be used to assess the children's knowledge and understanding linked to the objectives.

Using ICT to contribute to the 'wider curriculum'

Communication skills can be developed and consideration given by the children as to the best form in which to present their work. ICT skills can be developed and children can be asked to link the work on Muhammad to their own lives and what they have learned. This can be linked into the PSHE curriculum.

Summary

- ICT can support children learning about the Muslim faith and learning from it.
- Children can communicate what they have learned by using ICT applications and tools.
- The use of CD-ROMs and the Internet gives access to information and stories which can be used to support both teaching and learning.
- As children develop their ICT skills they can use an increasing range of ICT applications. These can include the use of multimedia presentations.

Unit 6E: What can we learn from Christian religious buildings?

This unit focuses upon Christian religious buildings and what can be learned from them. The link to the QCA scheme can be found at:

www.standards.dfes.gov.uk/schemes/religion/rel6e?version=1

Other useful sites include:

www.bobevans.care4free.net/ (an index of churches in and around Cardiff and information about various denominations, plus pictures)

eduwight.iow.gov.uk/curriculum/foundation/re/keystage2/ 3Unit_6E_.asp (a range of links to support planning, preparation and teaching).

In this unit the following objectives are given.

- What do we value?
- What do churches show about what Christians value?
- What can we learn from a visit to a Christian building?
- How can we deepen our understanding of the meaning of the place?
- How do buildings and objects relate to religious worship?
- How could we show what Christians value in a design for a religious building?

Your approach to this unit, as with the units on Jews, Hindus and Muslims, will depend on your personal knowledge and understanding. It may also depend upon the school in which you are teaching. If the school is a Christian faith school then you are likely to have access to a church and people who are willing to talk about their church. Wherever you teach there is almost certainly a church nearby which you can visit. First-hand experiences through a visit and the use of a 'knowledgeable expert' are very helpful and can generate interest for the children. The use of ICT can also be very helpful in supporting this unit and expanding the children's knowledge and understanding.

The teacher and ICT

This unit is designed to be spread over a number of weeks. It is up to you how you deliver the lessons to your class. Using the QCA scheme can help you to identify your teaching objectives, but you may vary what you teach according to the children in your class, their previous experience and the resources available.

In each section you can decide which present ICT opportunities for you or for the children. Suggested activities can have an ICT element to them and may be a way to develop or extend the children's knowledge and understanding of Christian religious buildings, whilst at the same time using ICT skills.

ICT opportunities

- The QCA scheme suggests that you identify with the children those things that are precious to them, or find words or pictures that have value. Give the children the task of finding pictures or writing words that meet the criteria. Using word-processing or DTP software they can integrate text and pictures and say why they have chosen the words, pictures or both. Their ideas could then be shared with the whole class through projected images and they could give reasons for their choices.
- Visit a church or churches near to your school. Check with the person in charge if it is acceptable to take photographs or video inside the church – these can be a useful resource in the classroom. Ask the children to add captions to the photographs or write brief descriptions of the place the objects have in the church and why they are important in Christian buildings. Images from work on other places of worship from different religions could also be used to look for similarities and differences. The use of 'virtual tours' mentioned earlier would further enhance the work.
- Use branching databases to identify similarities and differences. Set up more advanced databases so that children can identify different aspects of a church or collect data on artefacts that are important. The work the children have done on 'things of value' might also be included in the database and shared with others in the class.
- Use Paint, Draw or computer-aided design (CAD) packages to allow the children to draw churches they have visited. Alternatively, use the creative tools to design a church showing the main features of a Christian church. Choose a CAD program suitable for the age and skill of the children.
- E-mail is an effective way to communicate with an 'expert' or 'experts'. In this unit you will be looking at a range of churches

and whilst you will probably have an Anglican or Catholic church in the vicinity some other churches may be less accessible. Setting up e-mail links is one way of extending the children's understanding of different Christian churches. If your chosen 'expert' has the facilities, they may be willing to attach pictures to an e-mail so the children can see and discuss the differences.

- Software that enables multimedia presentation is an excellent way for children to produce work on such a topic. They can add sound, music, voice commentary, pictures, animations and video clips to their work. Children can talk over the presentation or can choose appropriate music to enhance their work.
- If your school does not have suitable hardware or software, the use of video recorders, CD-ROMs, tape recorders and OHTs can support the children's presentations.

Links to the QCA scheme of work

The list below identifies the main areas that could support this unit and presumes earlier units have been taught:

- E-mail (Unit 3E)
- Writing for different audiences (Unit 4A)
- Branching databases (Unit 4C)
- Analysing data and asking questions: using complex searches (Unit 5B)
- Evaluating information, checking accuracy and questioning plausibility (Unit 5C)
- Multimedia presentation (Unit 6A)
- Using the Internet to search large databases and interpret information (Unit 6D).

A LESSON PLAN: WHAT CAN WE LEARN FROM CHRISTIAN RELIGIOUS BUILDINGS?

Title
What can we learn from Christian religious buildings?

Year group
Year 6

Key questions or foci
- What parts of a Christian building are there? What aspects are important and why? What religious artefacts are found in churches and why are they important?

RE teaching objectives
- **AT1:** To learn about Christian religious buildings and how they may be similar or different. To learn about different parts of a church and the objects found there.
- **AT2:** To learn why churches and objects have meaning for Christians and why churches can be different.

ICT teaching objectives
- To use multimedia tools to communicate what they know about churches.

Learning outcomes – assessment opportunities

- **AT1:** To show evidence that they know there are different churches and how they are similar and different.
- **AT2:** To show they know why churches may differ and how those who worship there may hold different beliefs.
- **ICT:** To be able to use a software application to integrate text, graphics, sound and video and show evidence of what they have learned.

Resources

For teachers: digital camera, video camera, data projector, interactive whiteboard (or OHP and acetates).

For children: cameras, Internet access, Paint, Draw or CAD packages, multimedia software.

Lesson sequence

Introduction

Use presentation software to show the children pictures and text in order to focus the discussion, raise questions and share the objectives with the children. If you have a low level of ICT resources, use an OHP to display pictures and text. Reinforce the skills required to carry out the task.

Activities

See ICT opportunities (pages 67–68).

Conclusion

Ask the children to put together a multimedia presentation which shows what they have learned through a visit, or visits, to a church. Alternatively, the children use word-processing or DTP software to communicate what they have learned with text and graphics.

Using ICT to contribute to the 'wider curriculum'

As this is a Year 6 unit it provides opportunities for comparing the children's learning about Christianity with other religions and relates well to PSHE. Links can be made to the historical and geographical aspects of religions to help children understand the role religion can play in people's lives. Communication skills can be enhanced and ICT skills developed where the resources are available.

Summary

- Through 'virtual tours' ICT can give the children access to Christian religious buildings that they may not otherwise be able to visit.
- By Year 6 you would expect the children to have enhanced ICT skills which would allow them to use a range of applications and tools.
- ICT can support the children in independent learning.
- Children can use ICT to research information about Christian religious buildings.
- ICT can be used to support your own knowledge and understanding of the subject content.

Conclusion

This chapter has focused on four units from the QCA scheme for RE with ideas for supporting work with ICT. While there are many opportunities for first-hand experience, ICT can be used to support the knowledge and understanding 'about religions' you want the children to gain through your teaching. The use of the computer to support the children's communication is a positive use of ICT and can allow for the work to be differentiated to meet individual needs. Word and picture banks can support the children's writing without losing the subject focus for the lessons.

As the children progress through the school the potential for expanding their knowledge and understanding will be increased as they become more skilful at accessing and using a variety of ICT applications, tools and facilities. Your school may be developing a school website, or may have one already and information and children's work can be added. Software packages are now available that can translate work into a form that can easily be uploaded to the school's website. This enables children's work to be displayed to a wider audience (for more on this see Chapter 6).

5 Using ICT to support teaching and learning in primary citizenship

This chapter identifies the requirements of teaching and learning in citizenship at Key Stages 1 and 2. Citizenship is not a statutory requirement for primary schools and as such does not have a National Curriculum document to support your planning, but the QCA scheme and other documents do give a clear rationale for its inclusion in the curriculum. At **www.standards.dfes.gov.uk/schemes2/ks1-2citizenship/?view=get** the QCA gives an outline of how the scheme should be used and adapted to the needs of your children and your school.

This chapter takes a slightly different approach to those of the other humanities subject because the structure of the scheme does not relate the units to a particular year group but identifies the content as being developed through several years. The units chosen are as follows.

- Choices (Unit 2, Years 1–6)
- Developing our school grounds (Unit 6, Years 1–6)
- Respect for property (Unit 9, Years 3–6)
- In the media – what's the news? (Unit 11, Years 3–6).

A lesson plan outline is provided on p. 72 so that you can take content that you might teach with any of the year groups and incorporate your own objectives, activities and outcomes.

The main focus is on ICT to support teaching and learning, identifying the opportunities and how they can be put into practice.

It is important to understand that the knowledge may have to be approached from a slightly different perspective and involve more discussion, children's ideas, and a more 'open-ended' approach.

The following sites contain supportive information about teaching citizenship in the primary school:

www.teachernet.gov.uk/teachers/September2002/Whatiscitizenship_primary/ (background information, definitions and other links that you could find useful)

www.timeforcitizenship.com/default/index.asp?intro=tony&t=welcome (a wide range of support for teaching and learning citizenship and links to a Kids Zone, the emergency services, a teacher's area and an area for parents)

www.gloscc.gov.uk/teachers/curriculum/chap8.htm (support for citizenship and PSHE from the Gloucestershire Education Service; ideas and links are included)

www.standards.dfee.gov.uk/pdf/secondaryschemes/ks1-2_teachers_guide.pdf (guidance from the DfES on citizenship, from

Citizenship lesson plan

Information about the class/Why was this activity selected?			
Teaching objective/s (citizenship) *The children should know be able to:*	KSU ref	Learning outcome/s (citizenship) *I want evidence that the children can:*	
Teaching objective/s (ICT)		Learning outcome/s (ICT) – assessment opportunities	
Cross-curricular links:			
TASKS	USE OF ICT		USE OF ICT
Introduction:		Teaching points	
Activities			
Conclusion/review			
RESOURCES INCLUDING ICT:			
Teachers		Pupils'	
Organisation/differentiation/role of other adults in the classroom			

whole school ethos to planning and suggestions how it fits into the curriculum).

Citizenship and ICT

In the first three units we are going to look at ideas developed by the children whilst the unit entitled 'In the media – what's the news?' enables children to use secondary sources as the focal point for their learning. ICT can be used to support all of the units.

Where the children are learning about choices there is a clear focus on communication of ideas and discussing different points of view. ICT can support learning with a variety of applications and tools which enable children to be presented with different scenarios and can be used to share ideas and generate discussions.

Simple ICT tools can be used with younger children to generate posters on particular issues such as road safety, personal safety and issues relating to the school environment. More advanced use of ICT can be used by the older children linked to other subject areas. Work in science on healthy eating and lifestyles could be related to work on choices with ICT used as a support to learning. Sound pollution could be investigated with data-logging equipment and linked into areas of citizenship.

Work on improving the school grounds has the potential to use many ICT tools. Digital and video cameras, design software, word-processing and DTP software to integrate text and graphics are all possibilities. Using e-mail or writing and sending letters to communicate with 'experts' outside the school enables other ideas to be included in their thoughts and discussions. ICT can help children generate ideas and designs whilst consultations with other classes could be carried out electronically and ideas fed back through e-mail attachments.

The unit 'Respect for property' could be introduced by collecting pictures of the school or the local environment where vandalism has taken place, or where the environment has been neglected in some way. Children could use ICT to design posters that communicate a message about respecting the school and looking after it. Local spaces such as parks and buildings which have become vandalised or run down could be highlighted as potential areas for improvement. You could organise visits to local areas and photographs, digital pictures and video footage could record the problems and issues. Tape recorders and video cameras could be used to record the views of other children or those of local residents.

Word-processing software could be used to prepare questionnaires for distribution on how local people think the environment could be improved and vandalism reduced. Letters or e-mails to the local council and the police could elicit a response and show the children's concerns. From the responses, presentation software such as PowerPoint would enable a report to be prepared. A DTP package could be used to produce a newsheet to identify issues and make others aware of the problems. Organising the children into groups to take on the role of editor, photographer, reporter and computer user would facilitate the whole process.

'In the media – what's the news?' entails children having access to both local and national issues at an appropriate level. To be realistic, not all children you are teaching may read newspapers, watch or listen to the news. A visit to a local newspaper would help the children understand the different people involved and their roles and responsibilities when collecting news and producing a newspaper. The use of the Internet to access news reports is a way in which the children could be involved. Children could be taught about different ways the news is presented: newspapers, TV, radio and the Internet. School events could be reported to help children understand the process of news collection and publishing. Preparing a web page or part of a site helps children understand about content issues and enables children to be involved in making the decisions.

The next section of this chapter looks in more detail at the citizenship units and the role ICT can play in supporting the teaching and learning.

Unit 2: Choices

The web link for this QCA unit can be found at **www.standards.dfes.gov.uk/schemes2/ks1-2citizenship/cit02/ ?view=get**

In this unit there are four defined objectives for children to learn.

- What kind of decisions do I make?
- How do I make decisions?
- What influences our choices?
- How do we make informed choices?

Each objective gives you and the children the opportunity to discuss the issues related to each in turn. There are suggestions for looking at issues of:

- right and wrong;
- like and dislike;
- fair and unfair.

However, each issue can be based upon those things important to the children. Starting from the child's perspective enables issues and common features to be identified.

The teacher and ICT

The availability of an interactive whiteboard and associated hardware will enable you to 'brainstorm' ideas with the children, put them onto the board and save them for later discussions. This would be a useful 'starter' activity if you wanted to identify children's ideas. This approach could be used with any age group because it does not rely on the children's ICT skills as you will record and annotate. For example, you could prepare information about the school rules as they are, and then use these as a starting point for children's ideas and thoughts as to how things could be changed for the better. Adverts downloaded from the Internet could be a source for discussion, questions and answers. Once again the importance of your planning and preparation cannot be overstated.

ICT opportunities

- Show the children a list of words, descriptions or pictures describing or showing scenarios where things could be right or wrong, fair or unfair and so on. This could lead to a discussion with responses being sorted into categories and written up on the whiteboard. An interactive whiteboard or OHP would enable a whole-class approach whilst children could carry out the sorting activity on local computers or during time in the computer suite. The idea could be developed by asking children to explain the reasons for the choices they had made.

Helping children make choices
Scenario
You are walking down the street and find a £10 note on the ground. Do you:
1. put it in your pocket and say nothing to anybody?
2. take it home and tell your parents?
3. take it to your teacher?
4. spend it?

Each of the above statements can be linked to another page on which a further scenario is described. For example:

You have decided to put the £10 in your pocket and say nothing.
Do you think this was:
1. the right thing to do?
2. wrong, because it was not your money?
3. wrong, because you feel guilty?

Links are made from the other three choices with a further similar set of statements and so on. The links give children feedback and help them consider the choices they have made. They also allow for them to change their mind. Children can then share the process with others and this can be a focus for discussion and agreeing which would be the correct option.

75

- Software could be set up to give a particular scenario (as in the example). The children are given three choices. Clicking on a word or picture links to another page and moves the children through a range of options. The children can consider if the outcome is the one they expected and what they might do differently in the future. Older children may set up their own scenarios for other children to use.
- Use simulation or role-play software for children to build a storyboard with characters, events and descriptions. The children can build up an imaginative piece of work that involves decisions. This can then be used as a focus for whole-class discussion or as a stimulus for other children. The storyboards can be used in their own class, with other classes and other teachers or as part of an assembly. If specific software is not available, presentation software can be used to produce a series of slides as a storyboard. Kar2ouche is a software program that supports this approach.
- Children can communicate their ideas in a variety of ways: text, graphics, animations, sound and video. Each allows children to be creative and imaginative. Posters can be produced easily to communicate ideas. Software that allows the children to make animations from the simple to the more complex can motivate and enthuse. Where headphones and microphones are available children can add sound and commentaries to their work.
- Many of the units in the QCA scheme of work for citizenship lend themselves to children exploring themes and ideas through drama. Photographs, digital cameras and video are excellent ways to record the children's work.
- As part of literacy work children will learn about communicating to different audiences. ICT can facilitate this in a number of ways. Links to other children and other classes through e-mail can develop the idea of making choices on specific issues. Questionnaires might be distributed in this way and the ideas and data collected to inform decisions.
- School councils have been introduced into primary schools in the last few years and these can involve children in suggesting and making choices about aspects of school life. Ideas can range from school rules to improving the school playground and environment. ICT tools could be used to produce ballot papers for elections to the council. Council minutes could be saved and distributed electronically.

Links to the QCA scheme of work for ICT

The units you choose to use will depend on the age you are teaching and so specific units are not given here.

Using ICT to contribute to the 'wider curriculum'

Most teaching of citizenship will contribute to the 'wider curriculum' but ICT can enhance that contribution in a number of ways. Evidence of whole-class discussions and brainstorming can be collected, annotated and saved so that ideas are not lost. Children can be encouraged to communicate their ideas through a range of ICT applications and tools and their work can be supported by being able to access further information. With a range of software and hardware, work done away from the computer can be kept and shared in a number of contexts and at a level appropriate to the children's ability.

Summary
- The Choices unit is taught throughout the primary school. ICT can be used to support children at all stages.
- ICT enables children to communicate their ideas in a range of styles and formats and for a range of audiences.
- ICT can encourage children's creativity and imagination when considering choices.
- The use of ICT hardware can record children's work away from computers and be a focus for future ideas and discussion.

Unit 6: Developing our school grounds

The QCA link can be found at **www.standards.dfes.gov.uk/ schemes2/ks1-2citizenship/cit06/**

In this unit there are four sections, which focus on the following.

- How can we get involved in developing our school grounds?
- What do we think of our school grounds?
- What are priorities for improving the school grounds?
- Making changes.

Each section has related objectives, activities and outcomes, and asks children to consider wider issues of being part of a community and working with others.

The potential for using ICT within this unit is wide-ranging.

The teacher and ICT
The starting point could be to put together a video or photographic diary of the school and its grounds as they are now. This could be shown to the class or to the 'working group' if one were set up. Aspects that could be identified are:

- the playground;
- different areas for different activities;
- areas for the youngest children if the school has a nursery;
- quiet areas;
- wildlife gardens;
- areas for toys;
- storage.

Each class could be asked to look at the existing provision for the school as a whole and at specific areas that they use. ICT could be used to collect the children's ideas and produce a report showing what has been suggested to generate further ideas.

The cost implications could be put together on a spreadsheet by yourself or older children in the school. Paint, Draw and Design software could be used by children at the appropriate level to show ideas, which then act as the focus for discussion. Guiding children into considering the following aspects would be important:

- priorities;
- consulting;
- cost;
- raising funds;
- carrying out any work – who would be involved?
- timescale.

All of these have the potential to use ICT.

ICT opportunities

- Prepare a video of the school grounds along with photographs. The photographs could be shared with others in the school. If projects on developing the school grounds are initiated, a photographic record is a good way to keep a diary of developments. You could set aside an area on the school website to show the development of ideas and their implementation over time.
- Assign aspects of the development to different classes and specific ICT tasks to each at the appropriate level. A 'working group' of children and staff could collate ideas from different sources. Tape recorders could be used to record interviews about children's views, word-processing or DTP programs could be used to produce questionnaires for distribution, whilst the ideas of younger children may have to be collected and annotated by the teacher.
- Use software to generate ideas, identify priorities and create part of a whole-school display.
- Children in younger classes could use Paint or Draw programs to generate ideas such as making a wildlife area or producing areas for children to play games. Older children could use simple design programs to present their ideas. A whole-school competition could be arranged so that the best ideas are those that are adopted. ICT could also be used to produce plans.
- Once the designs, ideas and plans have been considered and agreed upon the children could, along with their teachers, consider issues of cost. The older children could use spreadsheets to show the costs for different aspects and decide on a list of priorities and timescale. ICT could be used to generate both of these.
- If costs have to be met through fund-raising activities the children can use ICT to generate and suggest ideas. Word-processing and DTP programs can then be used to advertise

specific events, whilst posters and 'flyers' could all be produced using software. The children can learn about writing for specific audiences and how to make an impact.

- Save all stages of planning, development and implementation. Children's writing in the form of diaries would be an ongoing record. Adding the presentation to the school website would be a useful way of keeping parents, governors and other interested parties informed.

Links to the QCA scheme of work for ICT
The units you choose to use will depend on the age you are teaching and so specific units are not given here.

Summary
- This unit could involve the whole school in making decisions about improving the school grounds.
- ICT can be used to identify various areas that could be developed.
- Children throughout the school can be involved in presenting ideas. Different software programs suitable for different-aged children can generate pictures, drawings and more detailed designs.
- Movie and still images can be used to record ideas, the progress of projects and as part of a final presentation.
- Children's ICT skills at different levels can be utilised to produce plans, spreadsheets of costs, posters, adverts and flyers for fund-raising events and a report of the activities undertaken and their views of how the school has been improved.

Unit 9: Respect for property

This unit could be integrated into, or developed from, the previous unit where the school grounds were the focus. The QCA unit can be found at **www.standards.dfes.gov.uk/schemes2/ks1-2citizenship/cit09/?view=get**

The main areas for children to learn are:

- the consequences of crime (stealing is wrong, victims of crime, consequences of shoplifting);
- lack of respect for school property;
- respect and responsibility for public spaces and problems of vandalism;
- buildings in the community.

The teacher and ICT
During the previous unit children will have explored the development of the school grounds. It is possible that the school has suffered from vandalism and this might have been part of the work. Inviting the police into the school to talk would be a possible way for you to introduce the unit. Alternatively, there are police videos that address

some of the issues. Widening the scope to vandalism could include the British Transport Police also who can provide speakers and videos.

Using photographs and video taken in the locality to identify areas where there has been vandalism or where public spaces have been subject to graffiti means you can focus the children's thinking. Reports taken from local newspapers and shared with the class would be a useful starting point for collecting children's views. Children could be asked to respond to questions about vandalism where they live, if they know anybody who has had their house broken into, and to consider aspects of behaviour that they consider wrong.

ICT opportunities

- ICT can be used to express views and opinions. Younger children can use text and pictures as their way of communicating. Older children may be taught and use ICT to produce multimedia presentations to identify the problems and suggest solutions by integrating text, graphics, sound and video. The children can be encouraged to think about different ways to present their views and information for maximum impact. They can consider the audience:
  - Is it for children in their class?
  - Is it for other children in the school?
  - Could it be shared with outside agencies such as the police or the local council?
  - Could it be shared with the whole school or their key stage through an assembly?

  The use of ICT can engage the children and involve them in the decision-making process.

- The use of familiar software enables reports to be written on any developments, achievements and future possibilities. Children can be involved in personal writing to present ideas and give their personal opinions on issues such as shoplifting, burglary and vandalism.
- ICT presents opportunities for children to be thoughtful, creative and imaginative. Paint, Draw and Design software allows children to present their own ideas on how people can have respect for property and what might discourage 'unsociable behaviour' which damages the appearance of public areas.
- Specific software is available that encourages children to look at particular scenarios and talk about them or produce their own storyboards. They can devise situations that involve characters carrying out certain actions and ask other children to talk about the issues. For older children such scenarios can involve discussions on rights and responsibilities.
- Word-processing or DTP software and email are ways in which the children can communicate with other agencies. The children can express their concern, detail what they feel and suggest

possible solutions. Using ICT in this way can help children feel involved in their communities – they can express their opinions and have others listen.

- Where questionnaires are devised to collect ideas from other children, the use of spreadsheets could be used to collate the information and block graphs generated to show those ideas and suggestions that have the greatest support. These could then be included in any report or in suggestions to outside agencies.

Links to the QCA scheme of work for ICT
The links below suggest those units which include the skills needed for the children to access the ICT opportunities suggested:

- Questions and answers (Unit 2E)
- E-mail (Unit 3E)
- Writing for different audiences (Unit 4A)
- Collecting and presenting information: questionnaires and pie charts (Unit 4D)
- Introduction to spreadsheets (Unit 5D)
- Multimedia presentation (Unit 6A).

This unit might be part of a school scheme where classes work together to collate ideas and draw conclusions. The lesson plan outline at the beginning of this chapter can be used and adapted for the age of children you are teaching.

Summary
- ICT tools and software can be used to identify children's existing ideas relating to respect for property.
- Pictures and videos of problems in the locality can identify problems and help children to discuss and consider the issues.
- Use of video provided by outside agencies can help children identify wider issues.
- A range of software can help children communicate ideas through text, graphics, video and sound depending on their ICT skill level and experience.
- ICT can enable children to be imaginative, creating ideas to change or stop those aspects of life which affect other people in a negative way.
- ICT allows children to communicate with outside agencies who have responsibility for the care and upkeep of property and the rule of law.

Unit 11: In the media – what's the news?

The QCA web address for this unit is **www.standards.dfes.gov.uk/ schemes2/ks1-2citizenship/cit11/**

Another site you might find useful is from the National Grid for Learning at **www.ngfl.ac.uk/QCAunits/Key** where there are a number of links for work on citizenship at Key Stages 1 and 2.

In this unit the objectives focus on:

- what's in the news;
- making the news – different ways of communicating information;
- how the media presents social issues.

Each of these areas, and the unit as a whole, offer potential for using ICT and can involve the children in presenting their own news in a variety of ways. The starting point could be 'what is meant by the news?' and how they find out about it. There are a number of different ways in which we can access the news with which the children may be familiar: newspapers, the TV and the Internet. Probably the most effective way to introduce this unit is to organise a visit to a local newspaper where children can see the news process for themselves.

The teacher and ICT
Introducing this unit to any one of the year groups could involve you in collecting a number of ways in which the news is presented:

- print;
- TV;
- radio;
- the Internet.

The focus for any one lesson could be based upon the objectives from the QCA scheme or ones you have identified yourself. The QCA identifies the following objectives:

- topical issues;
- local and national news;
- fact and fiction;
- the use of enquiry questions;
- evaluation of presentation;
- target audiences;
- different ways that information and news can be communicated;
- that the creation and presentation of information and news involves responsibility;
- to research, discuss and debate topical issues, problems and events;
- to explore how the media presents information;
- to work together in groups;
- to talk with a range of adults;
- to discuss, write about and explain their views on issues that affect themselves and society;
- that the actions people choose affect themselves and others;
- to try to see things from others' points of view;
- to use their imagination to understand other people's experiences;
- to create and sustain roles in a dramatic activity.

It would be best if these objectives were allocated to different groups at the appropriate level and to avoid duplication. Children in Year 3 could start with their own news. By Year 6 children could widen their knowledge and understanding by discussing issues of presentation and bias.

ICT opportunities

- This unit offers the potential for a range of ICT applications and tools. Text, photographs, digital images, sound and video are all possibilities.
- Encourage the children to communicate through a range of media. Use ICT to present the same story and ask children to compare the way it is presented, the ways opinions are expressed, and how opinions may be different. Interviewing the head teacher, other teachers or children about something that has happened in school could be used to help them understand various aspects of how the same story may have different perspectives.
- Produce a class or school newsletter with text and pictures. You could produce an electronic version, which can be placed on the school website. The children could take on specific roles: editor, photographer, writer and computer operator. The use of ICT can reinforce aspects of literacy work, such as writing for an audience, making an impact and drafting and redrafting stories.
- Children can write happy or sad stories, human or animal interest stories. Other types of stories could be identified from local newspapers. Children can identify which are 'good news stories', which need redrafting and which would not be interesting to the reader, listener or viewer. If it is not possible to use newspaper, TV or radio stories to identify issues, the school itself may present a number of opportunities.
- Software can be used to develop storyboards and address issues which might be important to the school ethos and policies.
- Where particular news stories have been identified, the children can use the Internet to access further information and see how news stories can change over time as more information becomes available. If the children's work is going to be put onto the school website they can look at how news websites present their information.

Links to the QCA scheme of work for ICT

Through this unit a range of ICT units can be addressed but particularly the following.

- Writing stories: communicating information using text (Unit 2A)
- Finding information (Unit 2C)
- Questions and answers (Unit 2E)
- Combining text and graphics (Unit 3A)
- Writing for different audiences (Unit 4A)

- Evaluating information, checking accuracy and questioning plausibility (Unit 5C)
- Multimedia presentation (Unit 6A)
- Using the Internet to search large databases and interpret information (Unit 6D).

Summary
- 'In the media – what's in the news?' presents a number of potential opportunities to use ICT. Not only do these enable children to meet the objectives for citizenship, but there is a great opportunity to develop ICT skills, knowledge and understanding in a real context.

Conclusion

In this chapter the units from the QCA scheme of work for citizenship are delivered in a number of years throughout the primary school. The approach you take to support the children's learning will depend upon how the scheme is implemented in your school. Teaching objectives, activities and outcomes may be allocated to specific year groups and this will influence what ICT applications and tools you choose to support teaching and learning.

In earlier chapters we identified the potential for using ICT with the proviso that the objectives for the subjects were clear and not masked by ICT use. When teaching citizenship ICT can support what and how the children learn and have clear cross-curricular links. ICT can be motivating and interesting and should involve the children in understanding what may be complex issues and outside their experience. ICT has the potential to bridge that gap.

6 Supporting ICT skills, knowledge and understanding

The aim of this book has to been to identify those aspects of ICT that could be used to support both teaching and learning in the humanities in the primary school. It has identified ICT opportunities and suggested ways in which you can support and deliver those opportunities. This chapter aims to provide a reference point for general issues that will support you and for the skills that you need to use yourself or teach the children.

You will be aware that there has been much in the media about the 'digital divide' between those children who have access to ICT at home and those who do not. You will need to take into account the skills children have and need before asking them to engage in ICT tasks. You should also be aware that school systems may not always operate in the same way as home computers. Your school system may have certain constraints upon it. Key Stage 1 children may not be given Internet access, whereas they may have open or selective Internet access at home. The children may be very familiar with saving their work to disk, the hard drive or to CD-ROM, whereas at school this might be limited by the space available on the server and the set-up of the school network. Ensuring that you, and the children, know the school protocol for ICT use will be important.

Despite a great deal of government money being invested in ICT in all schools during the last five years, the way that money has been spent varies considerably because of the 'baseline' from which schools started. Those who already had computers and Internet access may now be upgrading to broadband so that access to the World Wide Web is much faster and download speeds are increased. Many, but by no means all, schools have decided to put in computer suites, data projectors and interactive whiteboards. These types of development have an impact on the way lessons are delivered and how ICT can be used. If the school has a computer suite as the focus for ICT delivery you will have timetabled slots when you and your class can use ICT. In order to use ICT to support teaching and learning in the humanities you will have to make decisions as to how you teach the ICT skills required to those children who do not already have them. Even if your school is using the QCA scheme of work for ICT and you are teaching a Year 6 class, the scheme itself has not been in operation long enough to guarantee the children will have covered the units prior to you teaching them.

Interactive whiteboards lend themselves to whole-class teaching and presenting lessons with a high impact, but you should be careful that the 'wow factor' does not dilute what you want to teach. There is no doubt that using ICT requires a great deal of research and planning if it is to support teaching and learning in a way that other resources might not. The remainder of this chapter identifies general principles that underpin suggestions from previous chapters.

Skills

If you are a trainee or newly qualified teacher you need to show that you have the necessary skills, knowledge and understanding of ICT to meet the Standards for QTS. If you are a teacher in post you may have undertaken NOF training and if you are an LSA you will probably have been involved in supporting teachers in their ICT delivery. However, ICT has developed at such a pace that there are always new skills to learn and this involves time.

Time

You need time to:

- evaluate software programs and learn how best to use them;
- access websites that will support you as the teacher;
- identify and evaluate websites that children can use;
- put together materials and resources to introduce lessons – as with presentation software;
- prepare resources to support children's learning – as with word and picture banks, web trails and e-books;
- develop your knowledge of the school computer system and what it will and will not enable you and the children to do;
- develop your knowledge about the operating system used by the school;
- know about using ICT in a way that supports learning and does not impede it;
- consider how you might extend the use of ICT in the future.

Using software

Schools vary a great deal in the software applications they use for different aspects of the curriculum and each will have different tools, buttons and menus. You need to make sure you are familiar with any software you want to use. You may also be in the position to buy software to use with your class. Whether you are using software or purchasing it, there are some general 'rules of thumb' to consider.

- Is it easy to use?
- Will it be clear to the children what they have to do?
- Is it intuitive?
- Does the software allow the user to produce something quickly?
- Does it support learning in an interesting and motivating way?
- Is it cost-effective compared with other resources?

All software has a help facility, which gives support if you need it. Several primary packages now have video clips or animations to guide you through the basics of the program. There will also be a range of shortcuts to carry out operations such as saving, cutting, pasting and printing. It is always worth familiarising yourself with these as they can save you and the children time.

The following is a list of web addresses for software companies and manufacturers of peripherals, which would support the ideas presented in earlier chapters:

Software companies

In this section a number of software companies are identified who produce resources and CD-ROMs which would support teaching and learning in the primary humanities.

www.logo.com/
Longman Logotron produce a range of software relevant and appropriate to primary schools. This site describes the products.

www.microsoft.com/office/
Microsoft Office is probably the most well-known set of applications. This site gives support for using Office products.

www.kudlian.net/
Kudlian software is appropriate to primary schools with data handling packages suitable for both Key Stage 1 and 2.

www.textease.com/
Softease software is the manufacturer of Textease, which integrates a range of applications together. Textease Studio integrates databases, branching databases, spreadsheets, presentation, logo and other resources.

www.granada-learning.com/
Granada Learning has a wide range of software for primary schools with specific titles relevant to the teaching of the humanities.

www.rm.com/
RM Learning manufactures both hardware and software suitable for primary schools.

www.blackcatsoftware.com/
BlackCat software (part of the Granada Group) manufactures primary toolboxes and other software, which bundles suitable primary software together.

www.semerc.com/
Semerc software (part of the Granada Group) focuses on special needs.

www2.sherston.com/
Sherston offer a range of software to support both key stages in primary schools.

www.cricksoft.com/uk/
Crick software offer multimedia and communication software to support humanities teaching.

www.inclusive.co.uk/
Inclusive Technology is a software and peripheral manufacturer to

support children with special needs.

www.kar2ouche.com/

Kar2ouche software supports humanities teaching through multimedia authoring tools.

www.apple.com/quicktime/

QuickTime is downloadable software for viewing video on both PCs and Apple Mac computers.

Accessing the World Wide Web

Throughout this book the use of the Internet has been suggested as a valuable resource for you and the children. You can download information, pictures, sound and video as well as view materials online. This section supports the ideas described in earlier chapters.

The use of search engines for older primary children enables them to access a range of sites to support their learning. To help children carry out focused searches it is often best to set up sites in the *Favourites menu*. Some operating systems call this *bookmarking*. Another way is simply to copy web addresses on a particular topic area into a program such as Word, which can then be saved. When children want to access an address they open the document and click on the address and, as long as the computer is connected to the Internet, it will take the children direct to the site. This is done though *hyperlinks,* which are included in a number of common applications. A word or picture can be highlighted and the *link tool* used to set up a link to a particular site. The children can also be taught how to make a search using the URL *(Uniform Resource Locators)*. Links to sites in presentation software can be used to make your use of ICT focused and effective. If you do not have Internet access where you are teaching but want to show a page from a site, then you can download it to a laptop, a floppy (depending on the memory it takes up) or a CD. Clicking on the icon will show the page but will not allow you to navigate to other parts of the site. However, it does avoid delays in opening the page when you have the class in front of you.

Another aspect of using the web you should consider is the content of the sites you might want the children to use.

- Is it at an appropriate language level?
- Is the information easily accessible?
- Do you consider the information to be accurate, plausible and based upon evidence?
- Is it easily navigable?

On many sites, although not all, you can copy text and pictures. This allows you to make sure that what the children access has already been evaluated and deemed suitable. Text can be highlighted and copied and pasted into most word-processing or DTP documents, and pictures copied into a document or downloaded onto a disk, CD or the computer. (You may need to ask your ICT co-ordinator or system administrator if downloading is possible.) You may also need to e-mail a site to ask about any copyright on the content or restrictions on downloading.

Other aspects of Internet use

Some sites have useful video and sound clips as well as animations which can be used to highlight or teach specific aspects of a subject. You will need to make sure that the computer you or the children are using has the software to allow the clips to run. Real Player, Windows Media Player or QuickTime are the most common software for use with video although you might also need Java, Shockwave or Flash to run some movies or animations. If the software is not installed then a message will appear to let you know if it is freely downloadable. When accessing the Internet this will be done through a browser. It will help you to know what this browser is because you may, at some time, want to add what are called *plug-ins* for web pages to be displayed correctly.

Professional associations on the web
www.geography.org.uk/
The Geographical Association supports trainees, teachers in schools and higher education, advisers and inspectors. The site has links to information about the association, resources, events, projects and a shop.

www.history.org.uk/
The stated aims of the Historical Association are *'to further the study, teaching and enjoyment of history at all levels: teacher and student, amateur and professional'*. The site has a specific section for primary education where there are links to journals, resources and activities.

www.pcfre.org.uk/
The Professional Council for Religious Education is the subject teacher association for RE professionals in primary and secondary schools and higher education. The site has links to news, projects, resources, downloads and a range of relevant RE sites. There is also a section called *Children Talking*.

www.rmplc.co.uk/orgs/isrsa/syllabus/
The Independent Schools Religious Studies Association is a religious studies site aimed at those teaching in the private sector.

http://re-xs.ucsm.ac.uk/re-council/
The Religious Education Council of England and Wales seeks to represent the collective interests of a wide variety of associations and communities in deepening and strengthening provision for RE.

www.hums.org.uk/
The Humanities Association aims to provide an independent forum for debate about major issues in all aspects of humanities education. The site has links to news, events and resources.

www.naace.org/

The National Association for Advisers for Computers in Education supports all involved in using ICT in education.

http://acitt.digitalbrain.com/acitt/index.htm
The Association for ICT in Education is open to all those interested in the teaching of ICT and its co-ordination in schools.

www.itte.org.uk
The Association for IT in Teacher Education's aim is to promote the education and professional development of teachers in order to improve the quality of teaching and learning with ICT in all phases of education.

www.mape.org.uk/
Micro Computers and Primary Education describes its aim as supporting the effective use of ICT in primary education. MAPE gives support with curriculum, communications, software, management, reviews, hardware and links to other sites.

www.becta.org.uk/aboutsite/index.html
BECTa's site is designed to be a portal for ICT in education. It contains help, support and guidance and includes research reports, reviews and latest development. A must for all teachers.

Online links to government sites
www.nc.uk.net/nc/contents/ICT-home.htm4
The National Curriculum Online.

http://vtc.ngfl.gov.uk/docserver.php
The Virtual Teachers' Centre is a service for school professionals providing news, support for professional development and the facility to search quality-badged resources across the National Grid for Learning.

www.qca.org.uk/ca/5-14/gen5_14.asp
The National Curriculum and Assessment site gives guidance and help on the assessment of all National Curriculum subjects.

www.standards.dfee.gov.uk/schemes/
DfES site with links to the QCA schemes of work.

Website links to ICT in primary humanities

History
www.bbc.co.uk/schools/4_11/subjectsa_h.shtml#history
A range of online information, activities, games and other resources linked to the history curriculum.

www.britannia.com/history/h50.html
The Britannia site has a number of links related to the Anglo-Saxons. These include timelines, information on Saxon churches, and original documents.

http://historyonthenet.co.uk/

History on the Net aims to provide historical information linked to the English National Curriculum, for teachers, pupils, parents and anyone who wishes to further their historical knowledge. The site includes timelines, resources, lesson plans and other history-related materials.

www.holnet.org.uk/

This history of London site includes specific links to London during the Second World War and Victorian London suitable for Key Stage 2.

www.cidadevirtual.pt/poge/kings/pag1.html

A site showing Kings and Queens of England, their dates and graphics of their costumes.

www.activehistory.co.uk/3rds/ww2/home_front/intropage.htm

This site has an interactive game for children in which they make decisions. Active History also has interactive activities on memories of the Second World War, what caused the Second World War, and an 'Interview Adolf Hitler' section.

www.bbc.co.uk/education/dynamo/history/index.shtml

This BBC Dynamo site has a variety of interactive games linked to history. The games need Shockwave Flash 4, which is a free download.

www.mindwave.co.uk/vikings/index.html

The World of Vikings supports teaching and learning about the Vikings at Key Stage 2.

www.gwydir.demon.co.uk/jo/roman/index.htm

The Romans is a site with a range of information supporting work about the Romans.

www.gwydir.demon.co.uk/jo/egypt/

A range of information about Egyptian gods.

www.gwydir.demon.co.uk/jo/nordic/

Information on Nordic gods: a site that would support work on the Anglo-Saxons.

www.ancientgreece.com/html/history_frame.htm

A site to support knowledge and understanding of Ancient Greece.

www.j-sainsbury.co.uk/museum/museum.htm

Sainsbury's Archive Virtual Museum presents information about life in Britain between 1869 and 1900.

www.annefrank.nl/eng/diary/diary.html

A site dedicated to the *Diary of Anne Frank* giving an insight into her life during the war.

www.tudorhistory.org/
A site with information about the Tudor kings and queens. It includes graphics and supporting information for both teachers and children.

www.englishhistory.net/tudor.html
A Tudor history site with a number of original sources such as letters from the wives of Henry VIII as well as information, quizzes and portraits.

www.victorianstation.com/lifestylemenu.htm
A site dedicated to a range of information about Victoriana. There are sections on fashion, etiquette, leisure activities, recipes, day-to-day life and rituals.

Geography
www.naturegrid.org.uk/index.html
The Nature Grid site focuses on geography and science and has links to other sites, resources and relevant information.

www.topmarks.co.uk/
The Top Marks site allows you to search geography links depending on the age group being taught: Foundation Stage, Key Stage 1 or Key Stage 2.

www.nationalgeographic.com/
The National Geographic site is a useful resource for pictures, maps and other information related to geography areas you might be teaching.

http://uk8.multimap.com/
Multi Map gives access to maps of locations in the UK and countries and throughout the world.

www.upottery-primary.devon.sch.uk/RIVERS%20and%20 WATER
A site with links to a range of sites under the following headings: General, Maps and Atlases, Rivers and Water, Mountain, Weather, Environment, Habitats and Countries.

www.sutton.lincs.sch.uk/pages/weather/
Weather Station helps with studies on weather with links to reports, databases, activities, a quiz and a glossary.

www.foe.co.uk/
The Friends of the Earth website focuses on environmental and ecological issues.

www.meto.govt.uk/
The Met Office has a specific education section with a range of support information, materials and resources for teachers and pupils.

www.countrywatch.com/@school/
Country Watch is designed to help children learn about countries in an interactive way.

http://www.theodora.com/maps/abc_world_maps.html
A site with small GIF maps of the countries of the world to help children know and understand about place.

www.enchantedlearning.com/subjects/ocean/
This site gives information and answers questions such as 'Why is the sea salty?' There are also links to information about the water cycle, undersea explorers and other related topics.

http://officialcitysites.org/unitedkingdom.php3
Official City Sites has links to sites of many towns and cities in the UK as well as other internet links relating to the UK.

Religious Education
www.schoolassemblies.btinternet.co.uk/
A site where teachers can access and download ideas for school assemblies.

www.assemblies.org.uk/
A website specifically for primary school teachers, which allows teachers to access ideas for assemblies as well as submitting their own ideas.

www.schoolzone.co.uk/teachers/news/newsletter/issues/ 2002/April2002prim.htm
As well as ideas for assemblies there are links here to sections on religious artefacts, Bible stories, RE websites, Hinduism today, RE worksheets, Divali, Buddhist stories and other resources to support teaching and learning in RE.

www.theresite.org.uk/
This site has a number of links to support teaching and learning in RE.

www.halton.gov.uk/schintranet/weblinks/reforteachers.htm
A site with a range of links to other sites which usefully support teachers and where children can learn about and from religions.

http://members.aol.com/zippy2000/story/biblesto.htm
Links to a range of stories from both the Old and New Testaments, which could be read online, cut and pasted or shared with the children.

http://home.freeuk.net/elloughton13/dday.htm
A site dedicated to Divali, with stories and background information.

www.himalayanacademy.com/
This site gives a lot of information about Hinduism and how it is practised today. There are links to books, art, resources and a section called 'Basics'.

www.topmarks.co.uk/judaism/joseph/index.htm
This site has the story of Joseph and the story of Moses, both of which could be used when teaching about the Old Testament or the Torah.

Citizenship

www.bullying.co.uk/
This site is dedicated to helping all those involved in education understand the issue of bullying. The site has advice for teachers, parents and children as well as school projects, tips, links and a whole range of information.

www.citizen.org.uk/education.html
The Institute for Citizenship's site has a specific primary education section, which could support your work with children in both Key Stages 1 and 2.

www.oneworld.net/penguin/
The Tiki the Penguin site has links to topical issues, quizzes and fun pages. Focused for children to use but could be used by teachers.

www.streetwiseguys.co.uk/
Street Wise Guys has games and animated stories for children to learn about road safety.

www.hants.gov.uk/education/ngfl/subject/citizen/
The Hampshire Grid for Learning site provides a range of web links to sites that support teaching and learning in citizenship.

www.bbc.co.uk/education/id/
The BBC Learning site for citizenship has links and ideas for specific topics in citizenship at both Key Stages 1 and 2.

www.timeforcitizenship.com/default/index.asp?intro=tony&t =welcome
Your school can register at this site, swap ideas and gain further information to support teaching and learning.

Websites supporting the use of ICT in teaching and learning

www.ictteachers.co.uk/
A site that supports ICT teaching and learning in a range of subjects, including the humanities. There is a teacher's section and a Kids Zone.

www.educate.org.uk/cgi-bin/inetcgi/schoolsnet/home/ educate.jsp
Lesson plans, worksheets and other resources to support teaching.

www.ictadvice.org.uk/
Advice for teachers on using ICT to support teaching and learning, from BECTa.

www.teachingideas.co.uk/cgi-bin/adverts1/ads.pl?banner= adviva;time=1057515593
A site with a range of ideas for teachers, including using ICT when teaching the humanities.

http://vtc.ngfl.gov.uk/docserver.php
The Virtual Teachers' Centre is a portal to the BECTa software database, discussion groups to give you support from other

colleagues and TeacherNet. A link to the Teacher Resource Exchange gives access to other teachers' ideas for teaching, lesson plans and associated resources.

www.supporting-ict.co.uk/history.htm
A site linking the use of ICT to the teaching and learning of history. It has areas and links to support for both teachers and children.

www.teem.org.uk/
This site offers teachers' evaluations of a range of sites and software. It is very helpful in choosing appropriate ICT materials for your own use and that of the children.

Web links to publications and other resources

Geography
www.btinternet.com/~tonypickford/gg/tony.html
There are a range of resources at this site including recommended software and books.

http://vtc.ngfl.gov.uk/docserver.php?docid=1325
Planning for ICT and primary geography – a BECTa site.

www.leedsdec.org.uk/resourcesprimarygeography.htm
A range of packs and books from the Leeds Development Education Centre.

www.kented.org.uk/ngfl/prigeog/places3.html
Slides and other packs for supporting geography from Kent Education.

History
www.primaryhistory.org/go/Approach/TeachingMethod _177.html
Nuffield Primary History Resources.

www.learning-connections.co.uk/curric/cur_pri/invent/ res.html
Inventors and Discoverers – a range of texts to support this area of history.

www.hrp.org.uk/webcode/content.asp?ID=147
Historical Royal Palaces has both downloadable resources and publications for sale.

www.clickteaching.com/bookshop/history.shtml
Click Teaching has a range of publications and resources to buy, including EyeWitness books.

Religious Education
www.clear-vision.org
The Clear Vision Trust offers educational resources for learning and teaching about Buddhism.

www.iqratrust.org
The IQRA Trust offers educational resources for Islam.

www.bethshalom.com
The Holocaust Centre: exhibitions, resources and guidance on the Holocaust.

Resources for teaching Hinduism are available from Iskcon Education Services, Bhaktivedanta Manor, Letchmore Heath, Watford, WD2 8EP

Educational resources for Judaism are available from Jewish Education Bureau, c/o Rabbi Douglas Charing, 8 Westcombe Avenue, Leeds, LS8 2BS

Religious artefacts and resources are available from Articles of Faith, Resources House, Kay Street, Bury, BL9 6BU and Religion in Evidence, Monk Road, Alfreton, Derbyshire, DE55 7RL (sales@tts-group.co.uk)

Citizenship
www.citizen.org.uk/education/resources.html
The Institute for Citizenship offers free resources and publications.

www.wwflearning.co.uk/bookshop/cat_0000000015.asp
World Wildlife Fund: books and resources.

www.citizenship-global.org.uk/resources.html
A site with links to areas where you can obtain publications and free resources for global citizenship.

www.dep.org.uk/resources/Citizenship1-2/CitPriTeachbks.htm
Handbooks for teachers of citizenship at Key Stages 1 and 2.

www.oxfam.org.uk/coolplanet/teachers/links.htm
Cool Planet for Teachers: an Oxfam site with resources for teaching citizenship.

www.leedsdec.org.uk/resourcesprimarycitizenship.htm
Leeds Development Education Centre: a range of publications, books and other resources.

www.unicef.org.uk/education/educres.htm
UNICEF's resources for primary teachers.

ICT equipment

As you develop competence, confidence, skill, knowledge and understanding of how ICT can support your teaching and the children's learning there are certain tools that you may want to use.

- **CD/RW** stands for CD Read Writer and, if the computer has the facility, can be used to save text, pictures, video, sound and all aspects of work carried out on the computer. If you save work to a floppy disk it has 1.44 megabytes of memory whereas a CD has around 700 megabytes. This means that a lot of work can be stored on CDs and can avoid taking up computer memory. A child can save work done in school and if they have a CD reader at home they can continue work as homework.

- **DVDs** are becoming more and more common as a replacement for video players in the home. However, new computers and laptops often now have the software to enable you to burn DVDs or play them. These can be used to show children video clips, parts of films or play music. They are not yet common in primary schools but may be a useful tool for the future.

- **Data projectors** are becoming more common in primary schools and when used alongside **interactive whiteboards** they can enhance the teaching as well as the children's learning. They can be used for whole-class teaching but if fixed at the right height children can use them to show and talk about their work. Groups can also use them in conjunction with a computer or laptop to develop and enhance work they have done in a variety of contexts. The whiteboards have software which enables handwriting recognition, allows for notes to be written and saved, and for annotation. As these boards develop, other software will support teaching and learning in specific subjects. If you do not have a whiteboard it is still possible to project images on to a blank wall. The following sites give help and support in choosing particular makes or making the best use of whiteboards in your school.

www.promethean.co.uk/register.htm
Promethean is one of many manufacturers of interactive whiteboards who will give demonstrations of the possibilities that whiteboards oer in teaching and learning.

www.bournemouth-schools.org.uk/comparing_-boards.htm
Three of the most popular whiteboards are compared at this site.

www.kented.org.uk/ngfl/whiteboards/index.html
A project where teachers evaluate the use of SmartBoards and how they can support teaching and learning.

- **Digital cameras** have developed quickly over the last few years. They have the advantage that you do not have to wait for the film to be developed. Pictures taken by you or the children can be instantly put onto the computer and used to refresh the children's memory, referred to as a point of information or as a record of some aspect of a subject being taught. Some of these cameras have the facility for short movie clips to be taken (usually around 15–20 seconds) so that movement and voice can be added.

- **Video cameras** are still quite expensive, but the newer video cameras have digital facilities and *memory sticks* on which images can be stored and then transferred to the computers.

You will need the computer to have the memory and certain software to run the movie clips and the quality is improving all the time. If you are in a school with Macs they use iMovie to enable both viewing and editing.

- **Laptops and notebooks** have the advantage of flexibility. They can be used in the classroom as well as outside and on field trips. The development of wireless technology is still in its early stages and the cost may prohibit some schools from investing at the moment. However, where it is available it will allow children to use laptops and 'talk' to each other without the need for wires. Internet access can also be obtained with the use of wireless technology within a certain distance of a wireless access point.

- **School websites** are becoming more common as primary schools develop their ICT facilities. These can have children's pages to celebrate children's work as well as being a source of information for parents and outside bodies. Although some will still use HTML (*HyperText Mark-up Language*) to design the site, this would not be appropriate for primary children. However, there are primary software packages and more familiar applications on both PC and Macs, which will enable children to present their work for the school site. The software changes the work to HTML at the press of a menu button. Once this has been achieved the work can be submitted by using FTP (*File Transfer Protocol*) software.

The future

The possibilities that ICT affords in schools compared with five years ago has advanced considerably and it is difficult to assess what developments there will be in the next five years. One thing is certain – ICT will not stand still and many of the suggestions in this book would not have been possible in the past. What can be achieved with primary children still depends on their skills and your knowledge and understanding of the potential of ICT when supporting subject teaching. The debate about how ICT can be used to raise standards will go on until some empirical evidence links ICT with raising standards. What this book shows is that there are many opportunities for the use of ICT when teaching humanities subjects and these opportunities can be supported by a range of tools, applications and resources. Schools vary in the ICT they provide but, as was suggested in Chapter 1, it is when a high-level resource school uses ICT frequently and in a range of contexts that children's motivation, interest and learning improves.

ICT in the context of subject teaching and learning has much to offer but it does not operate independently. It is the teacher who evaluates and selects what, where and when ICT is most likely to support teaching objectives and learning outcomes. Planning and preparation is crucial, as is knowing the subject matter to be taught. The critical part is understanding how the use of ICT can be used to impact on your teaching and the children's learning. This book has aimed to support you in choosing and developing ICT in your context.

References

BECTa (2001) *Primary Schools of the Future – Achieving Today.* Coventry: BECTa.

BECTa (2002) *Connecting Schools, Networking People 2002, ICT Practice, Planning and Procurement for the National Grid for Learning.* Coventry: BECTa.

BECTa (2003) *Primary Schools – ICT and Standards: An Analysis of National Data from Ofsted and QCA by BECTa.* Available at **www.becta.org.uk/research**

DfEE (2000a) *National Curriculum Handbook for Key Stages 1 and 2.* London: DfEE.

DfEE (2000b) *Information and Communication Technology: Scheme of Work for Key Stages 1 and 2.* London: DfEE

DfES (2002) *ImpaCT2: The Impact of Information and Communication Technologies on Pupil Learning and Attainment.* London: DfES. Available at **www.becta.org.uk/research/impact2**

DfES/TTA (2002a) *Qualifying to Teach: Professional Standards for Qualified Teacher Status and Requirements for Initial Teacher Training.* London: DfES/TTA.

DfES/TTA (2002b) *Handbook to Accompany the Professional Standards for Qualified Teacher Status and Requirements for Initial Teacher Training.* London: DfES/TTA.

Moseley, D., Higgins, S. et al. (1999) *Ways Forward with ICT: Effective Pedagogy Using Information and Communications Technology for Literacy and Numeracy in Primary Schools.* Newcastle: Newcastle University.

Sharp, J., Potter, J., Allen, J. and Loveless, A. (2002) *Primary ICT: Knowledge, Understanding and Practice*, second edition. Exeter: Learning Matters.